Terrestrial Mammals of Nunavut

Published by Inhabit Media. Inc.
www.inhabitmedia.com

Inhabit Media Inc. (Iqaluit), P.O. Box 11125, Iqaluit, Nunavut, X0A 1H0
(Toronto), 146A Orchard View Blvd., Toronto, Ontario, M4R 1C3

Book design by Tony Romito
Design and layout copyright © 2013 Inhabit Media Inc.
Text copyright © 2013 Ingrid Anand-Wheeler
Cover image copyright © Patrick J. Endres/AlaskaPhotoGraphics.com

Photographs by Paul Nicklen (unless otherwise noted)

We acknowledge the support of the Canadian Council for the Arts for our publishing program.

Printed in China

Library and Archives Canada Cataloguing in Publication Data

Anand-Wheeler, Ingrid, 1971-, author
    Terrestrial mammals of Nunavut / written by Ingrid Anand-Wheeler.

Originally published as a bilingual edition with text in English and
    Inuktitut: Department of Sustainable Development, Nunavut, 2002.
Includes bibliographical references.

Published in partnership with Department of Sustainable Development, Nunavut
    Wildlife Management Board, and Quikiqtani School Operations.
ISBN 978-1-927095-74-4 (pbk.)

    1. Mammals--Nunavut. 2. Mammals. I. Nunavut Wildlife Management Board,
issuing body II. Nunavut. Qikiqtani School Operations, issuing body III. Nunavut.
Department of Sustainable Development, issuing body IV. Title.

QL721.5.N85A53 2014   599.09719'5   C2013-908450-9

Terrestrial Mammals of Nunavut

Written By

Ingrid Anand-Wheeler

Partners

Department of Sustainable Development
Nunavut Wildlife Management Board
Qikiqtani School Operations

Acknowledgements

Many people have made this book possible and I would like to extend my gratitude to all of them for their valuable input and support. I am grateful to the Department of Sustainable Development, Conservation Education Division, and Elise Maltin, as well as the Nunavut Wildlife Management Board and Jim Noble for partnering and making this project possible—and above all for allowing me the opportunity to write it. My thanks also go to Tony Romito for the incredible layout and design, Gwen Coffin for the literary edits, and to Evie Amagoalik for the translation. Thanks are also due to Lucy MacDonald, Andrew Qappik, and Paul Nicklen for their inspiring images, as well as the Igloolik Inullariit Elders Society, Igloolik Research Centre (John McDonald) ,and NRI for the traditional knowledge component.

I would like to thank the many DSD biologists who reviewed the species accounts and provided valuable feedback and corrections to the text and the range maps. In addition, my appreciation goes to staff at NWMB, RWED, and CWS for their assistance in various areas. I, however, assume responsibility for any error that may appear, whether factual or literary.

Ingrid Anand-Wheeler

Dedication

This book is dedicated to Manasie Audlakiak (1948–2013) and Winston Fillatre (1949–2013), members of the Nunavut Wildlife Management Board who truly personified the Vision of the NWMB: "*Nunavut: A world-class model for the cooperative management of healthy wildlife populations*." Manasie and Winston were particularly strong advocates of conservation education, and enthusiastically supported the development of this book. They would have been so pleased with the results.

Nunavut Wildlife Management Board

Table of Contents

Ingrid Anand-Wheeler, Author
Ingrid grew up in a small town on the South Shore of Montreal and was a homeroom teacher for three years before heading north in 1999. Two wonderfully rewarding years in Qausuittuq (Resolute Bay) helped further her teaching experiences and appreciation of small community living. Following this, she moved south to Iqaluit, where she began work on *Terrestrial Mammals of Nunavut,* thereby pursuing her interest in education in a different realm. Ingrid enjoys cooking, freelance writing, and amateur photography. She is a naturalist at heart and is happiest enjoying the beauty of the ocean and the outdoors in general. Ingrid lives in Iqaluit with her husband Ben and her dog Basal.

Lucy MacDonald, Illustrator
Lucy grew up in the community of Igloolik and attended Ataguttaaluk School. In 1992 she won a scholarship to represent the Northwest Territories at Lester B. Pearson College of the Pacific in British Columbia. After completing her International Baccalaureate there, she went on to study a Bachelor of Fine Arts with a minor in biology at Mount Allison University in Sackville, New Brunswick. In 1998 Lucy travelled to Scotland to attend the Edinburgh College of Art, where she completed a Master of Design in illustration. In 2000 Lucy returned to Mount Allison University to take the position of curatorial intern at the Owens Art Gallery.

Andrew Qappik, R.C.A., Illustrator
Andrew has been working as an artist for the past twenty years. He is a print-maker, an illustrator, and a sculptor. Among his many accomplishments are the Nunavut flag and the coat of arms. He has travelled widely, all over Canada as well as to Greenland and the United States. He would really like to encourage young people to try to achieve their goals. He has, himself, acheived his goals despite some bad, as well as good, times. "Do what you want to do," says Andrew. "It will be helpful to others."

Paul Nicklen, Photographer
Paul Nicklen grew up in two communities on Baffin Island, Nunavut, later moving to Yellowknife, NWT. In 1990 he completed his Bachelor of Science degree in marine biology at the University of Victoria. After spending the following four years working as a wildlife biologist with the territorial government on species such as polar bears, lynx, and others, Paul started his career as a professional photographer, specializing in the Arctic. After seven years of photographing full time, Paul's images have appeared in countless publications worldwide, including *Time, Life, Terre Sauvage, BBC Wildlife, Macleans, Canadian Geographic,* and *National Geographic.* For the past two years, he has been completing assignments for *National Geographic* magazine.

To all Nunavummiut,

The importance of wildlife to the people of Nunavut cannot be understated. For generations our people have relied on animals as a source of food, to provide clothing and shelter, and recently for economic benefits. While many people are familiar with Nunavut's "Arctic" big game species, such as polar bears, caribou, and muskox, not everyone is aware of the diversity of small mammals and furbearers that are also an important part of the territory's terrestrial wildlife. Furthermore, Nunavut's vast expanse encompasses a range of habitats, and along our western and southern borders, we have habitat that supports a number of species that are not as commonly thought of as "Nunavut" wildlife, such as moose, lynx, and bats.

This book describes the main species of land mammals found within Nunavut's borders, including their physical characteristics, behaviour, reproduction, diet, range, and status. This book is meant to be a general reference book for a classroom audience.

Terrestrial Mammals of Nunavut is the result of a collaborative effort between the Department of Sustainable Development, the Nunavut Wildlife Management Board, and Qikiqtani School Operations. It is the third in a series of Nunavut wildlife resource books, preceded by *Marine Mammals of Nunavut* (2001) and *Birds of Nunavut* (1997). This series was initiated to provide Nunavut students with easy-to-access information on territorial wildlife. It is with great pride that we introduce *Terrestrial Mammals of Nunavut.*

Honourable Olayuk Akesuk
Minister, Sustainable Development
Government of Nunavut

Family Name

Common Name
Latin Name

APPEARANCE

Describes characteristics of a species by which the animal can easily be identified, e.g., colour of fur.

FOOD AND FEEDING

Description of diet and feeding behaviours.

BEHAVIOUR

Describes the general behaviours of the species and explores aspects of migration, social behaviour, and use of specialized senses.

RANGE

Describes species distribution in Nunavut.

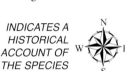

INDICATES A HISTORICAL ACCOUNT OF THE SPECIES

HABITAT

Describes ecological conditions required for life.

INDICATES A TRADITIONAL ACCOUNT OF THE SPECIES

REPRODUCTION

Describes how animals in a species mate and produce young.

STATUS, SURVIVAL, AND MANAGEMENT

Describes the status of the species in Nunavut, its future outlook, and the way wildlife managers control its use and protection, and identifies its main predators.

?

DID YOU KNOW ?

Describes interesting information about a species you may not have known before.

Artiodactyla

Bovidae
Cervidae

Muskox
Ovibos moschatus

APPEARANCE

A muskox looks like a great shaggy ox, but actually has more in common with a sheep or goat. The skull of the muskox is massive. The large, sweeping horns of an adult bull are joined together at the base and form a big *boss* that has many ridges on it. On a cow, the boss is smaller and is divided in the middle by a wider strip of white hair. The horn colour depends on age: pale in the young and shades of brown in adults. An underlayer of short, fine wool, called *qiviut*, covers everything except the horns, lips, nose, and hooves. A much longer outer coat made up of shaggy hair up to 62 cm long covers the muskox and makes it easy to recognize. The body colour is dark brown to black, with some cream coloured hairs on the back and around its feet. The *molt* begins in late April or early May, and at this time the muskox has a tattered look, with long pieces of fur blowing in the wind and small pieces of qiviut clinging to rocks and shrubs. Females are usually two metres in length and weigh between 280 and 295 kg. Males are generally two to two and a half metres in length and weigh between 260 and 400 kg. Rounded hooves with sharp rims provide traction on ice and rocky surfaces.

Paul Nicklen

FOOD AND FEEDING

Muskoxen are *herbivores* and feed on willow, tundra grasses, *forbs*, and seeds.

BEHAVIOUR

Muskoxen are social animals and live in herds with an average of 15 animals, although more or fewer may be possible. There is one dominant bull per herd and it is generally one of the larger males. This bull leads the herd in short migrations and when danger threatens. In all-cow herds, there is a cow leader that shows similar behaviour to the dominant bull. When threatened by wolves, muskoxen try to move to higher ground, where the dominant bull stops and faces the danger while the rest of the herd gather around him and form a characteristic line of defense. If there are young calves, they stay behind this line, or the adults form a circle with the calves protected in the centre. If the animals stay together, the intruder will most likely give up and look for easier prey. However, if one member gets separated the wolves then have a much better chance of killing it. Unlike caribou, muskoxen do not under-take long migrations, but in some areas they may have winter and summer ranges that are up to 160km apart.

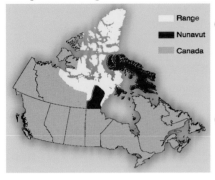

Range
Nunavut
Canada

RANGE

Muskox occur primarily on the Arctic islands in Baffin and northern Kitikmeot Regions.

HABITAT

Muskoxen live in the Arctic tundra and can be found in river valleys, lakeshores, and seepage meadows during the summer. In the winter, they shift to hilltops, slopes, and plateaus, where the winds blow the underlying vegetation free of snow.

REPRODUCTION

DSD

During the breeding season, referred to as the *rutting* season, the lead bull must always defend his position. The quiet of the Arctic is broken by the crash of muskox horns as the bulls challenge each other for the leadership of the herds and the right to mate with the females. The impact from the great blows is absorbed by the thickness of the horns and skull, and the weaker of the two usually moves on before much damage is done to either of them. Rutting peaks in the late summer and continues into September. Young bulls may try to re-join the herd, while older ones appear content to go off on their own and wander the tundra, eating and sleeping. After a *gestation period* of eight to nine months, usu-ally only a single calf is born; twins are rare. The calf stays close to its mother and within the safety of the herd for the first few weeks. As it grows, it moves around the herd's feeding area, playing with other calves. Whether a cow has a calf every year or in alternate years depends on geographic location and availability of food. In the higher Arctic islands the calf may feed from its mother for 15 to 18 months before being *weaned*.

STATUS, SURVIVAL, AND MANAGEMENT

According to the Nunavut Wild Species 2000 report, the current status of muskoxen is *secure*. They can live up to 20 or 25 years in the wild. Their predators in Nunavut include humans and some carnivores, primarily the wolf. Their numbers dropped dramatically due to overhunting at the turn of the 19th century. In 1917, realizing that the animals were in danger of being completely exterminated, the Canadian government prohibited the trading of hides and put muskoxen under complete protection. Since that time, their numbers have increased and hunting is allowed. A *sustainable harvest* is maintained through a quota system.

DID YOU
KNOW ?

Muskoxen can and will swim to evade wolves or simply to cross a river. Some Inu refer to them as *oomingmak*, which means "the bearded one."

Apparently the Musk-ox is seldom if ever found in the region of western Coronation Gulf around the mouths of Rae River, Richardson River, or the lower portion of the Coppermine River. Quite a number of Eskimo hunt in this region, and they say that the Musk-oxen are all farther to the east. Some old men in the Rae River region had never seen a Muskox. The number of Musk-oxen now living west of the lower Coppermine River is very small and probably confined to the rather small area of high, rocky barrens comprised in the triangle whose apices are Darnley Bay, Coronation and the north side of Great Bear Lake. From all the information we could get from the Coronation Gulf Eskimo, Musk-oxen are seldom if ever seen near the mainland coast less than seventy-five miles east of the mouth of the Coppermine River. It seems probable from information which Mr. Stefansson received from numerous groups of Eskimo in Coronation Gulf, Dolphin and Union Straits, and Prince Albert Sound, that no Musk-oxen at all are found in either the southern or central portions of Victoria Island (i.e. Wollaston Land, Victoria Land, Prince Albert Land). Some of these Eskimo remember of the former occurrence of the Musk-ox around Minto Inlet and Walker Bay, but say there are now none in that region. It is their belief, however, that Musk-oxen are still found near the north coast of Victoria Island. Musk-oxen are said to be still common on Banks Island. The Muskoxen are so readily killed, often to the last animal in a herd, that the species cannot hold its own against even the most primitive weapons, and the advent of modern rifles means speedy extinction.

Anderson, 1924

Barrenground Caribou
Rangifer tarandus groenlandicus

APPEARANCE

Barrenground caribou are medium-sized cervids that have adapted to a life spent in the cold, walking great distances over snow and soggy tundra. They have large, well-furred *muzzles* and short, broad, furred ears. The coat is made up of a fine *under-fur* covered by long, coarse, hollow *guard hairs*. There is some variation in colouring, not only during different seasons, but between various regions across Nunavut and occasionally within a herd of animals. During summer the back, chest, and face are mostly brown. In the autumn, the lighter winter fur begins to appear, and by winter the animals are usually much paler. The neck is cream coloured and the belly and rump are white. Both males and females have antlers, but develop and shed them at different times during the year. Adult bulls usually shed their antlers in November or December after mating, whereas cows and young animals often don't shed their antlers until late winter or spring. Pregnant cows usually retain their antlers until calving in June. On the mainland of Nunavut, adult males weigh an average of about 150 kg in the autumn, while females average about 90 kg. Barrenground caribou on the southern Arctic islands of Nunavut usually weigh somewhat less, depending on the available forage. Adult males can lose 30 percent of their maximum weight during the fall *rut*. Females may lose 10 to 20 percent of their weight by late winter.

Paul Nicklen

FOOD AND FEEDING

The barrenground caribou feeds on a wide variety of plants, but the availability of lichens is most important for maintaining a healthy body weight and overall survival. Caribou that winter in the forests south of Nunavut eat a large amount of lichens. Special bacteria, protozoa, and other organisms in the caribou's stomach allow it to digest lichens and other forage properly. The caribou has successfully adapted to the Arctic and has little competition from other animals for lichens. The barrenground caribou also eats grasses, sedges, mosses, *forbs*, willow leaves, twigs, and mushrooms. It may sometimes chew on old discarded antlers, eat seaweed, and lick salt deposits in the ground and fresh sea ice, likely for the mineral content. There are rare reports of caribou consuming lemmings, Arctic char, and bird eggs.

BEHAVIOUR

Barrenground caribou are social animals that travel in herds of 10 to 50 animals, or loose bands of 1,000 on the mainland. Large groups are rarely if ever seen on the Arctic islands. For most of the year, the bands are generally made up of like individuals—for example, bands of adult bulls or bands of cows, their calves, and yearlings. Immature males may associate with either adult bulls or cows. Generally, the different age and sex groups only join together during the *rutting* season, although they interact at other times. The groups are almost always on the move from one seasonal pasture to the next and the leadership changes often. Some of the seasonal migrations can be as far as 1,200 km. On the Arctic islands some animals migrate 500 to 750 km, while others migrate less than 25 km, depending on the location of seasonal habitats. Pregnant cows, anxious to get to the calving grounds, usually lead the herd to the summer grounds. Adult bulls rarely complete this migration and stay closer to their wintering areas instead. On the mainland, herds are named after the feeding and calving grounds to which they migrate annually. On the islands, caribou populations show different migratory behaviours. No matter the distance, their migrations take them across many rivers, and fortunately, caribou are excellent swimmers. They float high in the water with much of their backs exposed, using their broad hooves to propel themselves. Caribou are generally quiet animals, but when they are surprised, or perhaps annoyed by insects, they snort loudly. Calves that have been separated from their mother call for them by making a deep grunting sound. Caribou have a great sense of smell and depend on it to detect both food and danger. Their hearing and eyesight are average. Predators can usually get quite close if they are upwind and haven't been spotted, but the average caribou can outrun a wolf.

RANGE

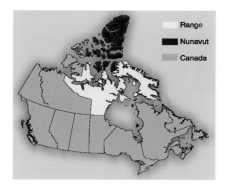

Range
Nunavut
Canada

Barrenground caribou are found throughout the mainland in Kivalliq and Kitikmeot Regions and most of Baffin, Victoria, and Southampton Islands, as well as several smaller islands in the northern and eastern Foxe Basin. On the mainland, the Qamanirjuaq, Beverly, Bathurst, and Bluenose herds winter in the forests south of Nunavut, while population on the northern mainland and arctic islands occupy Nunavut's tundra year-round.

HABITAT

As is suggested by its common name, these caribou live on the barren land or tundra of northern Canada. In the summer, mainland caribou search for snowy patches in order to escape the heat and mosquitoes. During the winter, they seek out rugged terrain, where patches of bare, windblown tundra allow access to forage and slopes where there may be some shelter from high winds.

REPRODUCTION

Barrenground caribou breed in the autumn. Like most deer species, males compete vigorously to breed, at times leading to weight loss, injuries, and perhaps lower chances of survival. Calving times vary depending on geographic location, but are generally during the month of June and may continue into early July. Following a *gestation period* of 7.5 to 8 months, one calf is born. As the time approaches for the cows to give birth, they separate from other animals and give birth, often on or near a patch of snow. At birth, the fawns measure about 60 cm in length and weigh about 5 kg. Mothers lick the newborns clean and eat the placenta and other newborn tissues. The young can usually stand up shortly after birth and are able to run a few miles after only 90 minutes. Within two days, they are able to keep up with their mothers. They begin nursing when they are a couple of hours old and may continue to do so occasionally into the winter. *Weaning* usually occurs in late August or September.

STATUS, SURVIVAL, AND MANAGEMENT

According to the Nunavut Wild Species 2000 report, the status of barrenground caribou is *secure*. Mortality is high in the first year of life, but adults live about 5 to 10 years. Some caribou live up to 16 years. Their main predators in Nunavut include humans and wolves. Lichens can store high levels of *radioactive fallout*; although the levels of contaminants found in caribou have decreased in recent years, there remain concerns about the possible effects on humans, because caribou are an important source of food in Nunavut. Barrenground caribou have gone through massive long-term population fluctuations in the last 100 years. Inuit often view these changes as cycles with a peak and declining period, generally lasting the lifetime of an elder (about 60 to 70 years).

OTHER SPECIES IN NUNAVUT

There is an ongoing debate as to how many subspecies of caribou exist. It is generally accepted that barrenground and Peary caribou are different subspecies to the main species of caribou and reindeer. The caribou found on the Belcher Islands and Sanikiluaq are reindeer that were introduced in 1978 from a semi-domesticated herd in the NWT.

Peary Caribou

DID YOU
KNOW ?

After a few days, a young fawn is able to outrun a human being and swim about 135 m. Upper *canine* teeth are generally found in males and females; however, they remain unused and below their gums. This indicates that at one time the caribou may have had a use for canines. This is a great example of the *evolutionary process* that organisms may go through.

Noah Oqaituq

Belcher Island Reindeer

George Kappianaq shares his knowledge with regard to hunting caribou at water crossings.

There are lakes and rivers where caribou were hunted as they were crossing the water during migration. It was forbidden to catch caribou on the side where they entered the water. It was said that if such a thing were practised, caribou would not travel through that place again. Even though they were not around at the time of the kill, future caribou would refuse to travel the route where the caribou was killed. This happened if a caribou had been butchered, especially along the shore area. The solution was that the hunters would hunt caribou on the opposite side of the lake or river that the caribou entered from. They were very careful not to kill caribou on the wrong side. That was one of the things that we were discouraged from doing. In the event that a caribou was caught on the entry side, they had to make sure that there was no blood spilled or entrails left on the kill site.

At this time it was difficult to get implements for hunting. The only way they would be able to catch caribou in numbers was when the caribou were swimming across a lake or river, in the calmer flows. The hunters would wait for the caribou to start swimming. Once the caribou were well in the water and could not swim back quickly, hunters would pursue them in a qajaq. They would be killed in the water by lancing them. Then they would tow them to the other side where their tents were pitched, not to the side where the caribou had taken to water. This was the case where the caribou were hunted in lakes.

George Kappianaq, 1997

Peary Caribou
Rangifer tarandus pearyi

APPEARANCE

Peary caribou are the smallest North American caribou. During the winter, they have a thick coat of white fur. Their summer coat is short and dark, often paler than barrenground caribou. Their thick coats are made of hollow hairs that help trap warm air and insulate their bodies. Unlike most species in the family Cervidae, both male and female caribou have antlers. While growing, the antlers are covered with skin and dense, velvety, grey hairs. The skin contains blood vessels, which nourish the long bone growing underneath. The bulls' antlers begin to grow in March and are full grown by August. In September, males begin rubbing off the velvet, and by October their antlers are clean. By February most bulls have lost their antlers. Cows' antlers grow from June to September and the velvet stays on until October. They usually drop them between April and June. As with many other caribou, Peary caribou have short, broad, well-furred ears, large, crescent-shaped hooves, and large, furry *muzzles*. Females weigh an average of 60 kg and are about 1.4 m long. Males weigh an average of 110 kg and are generally 1.7 m long. However, the weight of Peary caribou varies greatly depending on geographic location, season, and availability of food.

Paul Nicklen

FOOD AND FEEDING

Purple saxifrage is one of the Peary caribou's favorite plants, and in June their muzzles may become stained purple. Because of the limited *biomass* of plants in their range, Peary caribou will eat almost any food available, like grasses, sedges, lichens, willow, saxifrage, and mushrooms. They have a keen sense of smell and use it to detect food under the snow. Their sharp, shovel-like hooves allow them to dig or crater through the snow to find food; however, some seem to find food mainly where the wind has blown snow away. Deep snow, ice-covered ground, and wind-packed snow may create difficult feeding conditions. In winter, Peary caribou seem to prefer habitats where both grasses and lichens occur, although lichens are of limited availability.

BEHAVIOUR

Although they do not undertake lengthy seasonal migrations compared to the barrenground caribou, Peary caribou do migrate between summer and winter ranges, sometimes moving between islands—up to 150 km each way. While the muskox uses defence circles against predators like wolves, Peary caribou use their speed to escape to high or rugged ground. In good conditions

Paul Nicklen

a caribou can usually outrun a wolf. The Peary caribou, like other caribou, are great swimmers. They use their large, shovel-like feet to propel themselves. Peary caribou are generally found travelling in small groups, grazing along the way. In winter usually only one to four Peary caribou are seen together, probably an adaptation to the small patches of forage that are available. Since very large groups of barrenground caribou gather when and where insect pests are common, the rarity of High Arctic mosquitoes may partially explain why large groups of Peary caribou have not been observed. In summer, groups commonly range from 1 to 12 caribou.

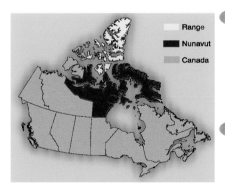

Range
Nunavut
Canada

RANGE

The Peary caribou can be found on the High Arctic islands, including Prince of Wales, Somerset, and the Queen Elizabeth Islands.

HABITAT

During the summer, Peary caribou are found on the upper slopes of river valleys and uplands where the vegetation is richest. During the winter, they inhabit areas where the snow is not too deep, such as rugged uplands, beach ridges, and rocky outcrops.

DSD

REPRODUCTION

Male Peary caribou can reach sexual maturity in their second year and females in the third. If a female has been able to build up enough fat reserves over the summer, she will mate sometime in the fall. After a *gestation period* of 7.5 to 8 months, one calf is born. Calf survival depends on the ability of the mother to produce milk in the post-natal period. In some severely cold years, most calves in a population may not survive. However, the long-term survival of populations depends more on the survival of the females and their ability to breed in following years.

STATUS, SURVIVAL, AND MANAGEMENT

According to the Nunavut Wild Species 2000 report, the status of Peary caribou is *sensitive*. Peary caribou may live 15 years in the wild, but rarely do. Various studies and recovery projects are underway to ensure the continued survival of the Peary caribou. One population of Peary caribou crashed in the mid-1990s after increasing to peak levels in the 1980s and early 1990s. A survey by biologists and local hunters in 2001 showed that the population had started to recover. The Inuit of Resolute Bay have restricted their harvesting of this population since 1975. Their efforts to conserve the Peary caribou have been recognized by the Wildlife Society, the world's largest association of wildlife biologists and managers.

OTHER SPECIES IN NUNAVUT

The existence of the "Arctic islands" caribou is an ongoing debate, not only among scientists but among traditional knowledge supporters as well. Some believe that this species is different from both barrenground and Peary caribou, while others do not believe the differences are great enough to distinguish them as a subspecies.

The name caribou comes from the Micmac name *xalibu*, which means "the pawer" and refers to the caribou's habit of pawing the ground to uncover lichens. The Peary caribou was named after the man some believe was the first to reach the North Pole; however, the northern limit of Peary caribou is 800 km south of the Pole.

Aipilik Innuksuk remembers methods of drying caribou back sinew and some of its uses.

The caribou back sinew was stretched to dry by some women, but I did not find it best that way. When it was stretched too much it would not make good strands and would break off easily. When it was stretched just enough it would not break easily. You had to stretch it to some extent but not force it. Niulirnngait, caribou leg tendons, were treated the same way as the back sinew. You just laid them straight to dry.

You could bite on the Niulirnngaq to prepare it to make strands out of it. This kind of sinew was used for tougher jobs like sewing extra soles for kamiks, sewing harpoon lines, dog traces, and so on, but it used to be braided. It could also be used as laces for kamiks. You could make a long braided strip by adding another strand as you braided it to make it longer and longer. One tendon could make a very long piece. One time I was braiding one and I said to my Uumaaq, "I braided this well, you could attempt to break it but you could not possibly break it!" So he tried and he did break it!

These could be used for Amauti belts but they are not good for Qulittaq, because the surface is rough and therefore they pull the hair off the Qulittaq. We used skin ropes for our belt because they do not pull the hair off.

One tendon produces a strand of ten to twenty feet. It is handy to have a supply on hand just in case you need some one-day. One time someone saw me braiding one and suggested that I should sell the ones that I braided, I said no because they were for Inuit use.

Aipilik Innuksuk, 1986

Moose
Alces alces

APPEARANCE

The moose is the largest member of the family Cervidae, which also includes caribou and deer. It has a long head with a hanging, rounded nose and a strip of fur dangling from its neck that is called a *dewlap*. The moose's coat ranges from reddish-brown to black. It has very long, greyish legs, with some white on the inside of the legs and stomach. Males have large, flat, shovel-shaped antlers with small points at the ends. These fall off every year and new ones grow to replace them. Females are usually between 2 and 2.6 m long and 330 to 396 kg. Males are usually between 2.3 and 2.8 m long and weigh 385 to 816 kg.

FOOD AND FEEDING

Paul Nicklen

Moose are *browsers*, and in the winter they feed on twigs, shrubs, and the bark from saplings. In the summer they feed on leaves, large quantities of salt-rich water plants, *forbs*, grasses, and foliage. By the time spring arrives, the moose's salt reserves are very low.

BEHAVIOUR

Moose seem to be the least social of all the ungulates and are mostly solitary animals. They are shy and will generally flee from humans. However, mothers are very protective of their young and will charge at intruders to chase them off. In the mating season, bulls are dangerous. Moose show some activity during the day, but are most active at dawn and dusk. During the summer, they are most active on calm, cloudy days following a storm.

REPRODUCTION

During breeding season the female is quite vocal as she calls for a male. Mating takes place in the autumn and after a *gestation period* of between 7.5 to 9 months, usually one calf is born, although at times twins and very rarely triplets occur. The young stay with their mother for a year and go off on their own in the spring before she gives birth to the next litter. Females and males reach maturity at two to three years of age, but males generally do not have the opportunity to mate before they are five or six years old. Moose can live up to 27 years.

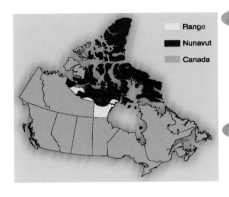

RANGE

In Nunavut the moose can be found in the southern portion of Kivalliq Region and in some parts of southwestern Kitikmeot Region.

HABITAT

Moose are found in wooded areas, swamps, lakeshores near forests, muskegs, streams of great boreal forests, and tundra areas.

STATUS, SURVIVAL, AND MANAGEMENT

According to the Wild Species of Nunavut 2000 report, the current status of the moose is *sensitive*. Moose may live up to 27 years. Their main predators in Nunavut include humans and some carnivores. They are hunted throughout Canada and were reintroduced in parts of eastern Canada following extinction due to overhunting.

DID YOU KNOW ?

Moose antlers are among the largest of all animal antlers; some may stretch to 1.8m and weigh almost 32 kg.

The Moose is common throughout the timbered country all along the Mackenzie River, and has occasionally been seen north of the timber line near Richard Island. According to the opinion of old residents and to data collected by the expedition, the Moose is increasing all through the northern country as well as extending its range rapidly and noticeably. A Coronation Gulf Eskimo from the region near Rae River (Pal'lirk) told us that he had seen two Moose (which he thought cows, from their small antlers) near the mouth of Rae River in 1909 or 1910. These Eskimo often hunt in summer down to Great Bear Lake and know the Moose from that region. Rae River flows into the southwestern corner of Coronation Gulf, and the Moose undoubtedly wandered here from the region around Great Bear Lake.

Anderson, 1924

Carnivora

Canidae
Felidae
Ursidae
Mustelidae

Grey Wolf
Canis lupus

APPEARANCE

The grey wolf looks a lot like a sled dog but it has longer legs, bigger feet, and a narrower chest. It varies in colour from snow white to jet black and can be all shades of grey, cream, brown and orangey-black. Different-coloured pups can come from the same litter. White is the most common colour for the Arctic islands, and dark colours dominate in forested areas. The wolf has a thick coat made up of long, rough *guard hairs* and short soft *under-fur*. Females weigh between 30 and 35 kg and are 1.4 to 1.8 m long from nose to tip of tail. Males weigh between 35 and 40 kg and are 1.5 to 2 m long from nose to tip of tail.

Paul Nicklen

FOOD AND FEEDING

Wolves feed mainly on big game, but what kind depends on their habitat. Wolves that live on the tundra feed mostly on caribou and muskox, depending on availability. Within the tree line, they hunt bison, moose, deer, and caribou. Although wolves hunt mostly big game, their diet changes with the seasons and the availability of food. It may also include hares, foxes, small rodents, beaver, fish, birds, eggs, and even small amounts of grasses or other vegetable matter.

BEHAVIOUR

Wolves are very social animals and have a complex *hierarchy* within their pack structure. There is generally a dominant or *alpha* pair in every pack. This pair will mate and every member of the pack will help them raise the young pups. The size of the pack depends mainly on the availability of food. A pack is usually made up of one set of parents with their pups, and sometimes an aunt or an uncle as well. At times, an unrelated wolf may be allowed to join the pack. There are a few reasons why lone wolves may have *dispersed* from their original pack. They may be looking for food, perhaps they are looking for a mate to start a pack of their own, or it could be that they were not getting along well with the other pack members. Wolf packs travel, hunt, breed, raise pups, and in most cases take care of a home territory together.

During the winter, they travel long distances together, hunting where they find prey and resting when they are tired or the weather turns nasty. In the summer, the wolves will go out hunting, but will always return to the *rendez-vous* site. Wolves are known to howl alone and with others for different reasons. A howl may be a call for adults to get together and hunt, or a way to find a lost pup. It might also be that wolves just like to howl. People who have watched wolves howling say it looks like they are having fun. Wolves have a great sense of smell and excellent hearing, but their eyesight is not as keen. Wolves use the same dens for generations, unless they are disturbed, in which case they abandon the den completely and never return to it.

Range
Canada

RANGE

Grey wolves are found throughout Nunavut.

HABITAT

Wolves show little preference for special habitats. They are found on the Arctic tundra and on plains, as well as in forests in their southern ranges.

REPRODUCTION

Female wolves come into heat once a year for about five days in late winter. At this time, the wolves are very active and social, which means there is a lot of howling. The *gestation period* is about two months, and how many pups are born between May and mid-June depends on the amount of food available and on geographic location. A bitch can have anywhere between 2 and 10 pups per litter. At birth, the pups are blind and deaf. They weigh about 0.5 kg and are completely dependent on their mother. For the first three weeks of life, the pups stay in the den, stumbling about, slowly discovering the inside of the den as their senses develop. Soon after, they begin exploring the entrance to the den and the outside world. A pack might move the pups to a different den, but otherwise the pups do not travel very far during their first summer. Making sure the pups are well fed takes a lot of time and the pack is very busy during the pups' first summer. They have been known to travel hundreds of kilometres in search of food for the pups. They either carry the food back in their mouth or it is swallowed and carried in the stomach, which acts like a packsack. When the parent or any other pack member arrives back at the den, the pups lick at the corners of their mouths so that they bring the food back up. Some pack members stay at the den babysitting the pups

Paul Nicklen

when they are young. When the pups are about two months old the pack may leave the den and move to a *rendez-vous* site, where they rest, play, and feed until the young are big enough to travel. The pups develop strong bonds with the pack. A wolf family may stay together for many years, hunting and travelling as a pack. Although pups are born most years, the pack size does not always increase quickly, as many of the young do not survive their first year. When wolves reach maturity and are ready to mate, they may *disperse* and go in search of a new pack or a partner to start their own pack.

STATUS, SURVIVAL, AND MANAGEMENT

According to the Nunavut Wild Species 2000 report, the current status of grey wolves is *sensitive*. Grey wolves generally live 10 years in the wild and up to 18 in captivity. In Nunavut, predators include humans, and pups are vulnerable to bears and raptors. Wolves are mostly hunted for their fur, which is used to make clothing. Many scientists believe that wolf populations can only be as healthy as the populations of their prey. For example, if caribou are in decline, this might have a direct impact on the wolf populations.

DID YOU KNOW ?

Scientists continue to debate whether there is a difference between Arctic island wolves, tundra wolves, and timber wolves. Wolf skulls from different regions are sent in and the *DNA* is analyzed to see what differences and similarities there are between these wolves in order to help them identify any subspecies.

Noah Piugaattuk remembers how the wolves once warned travellers of impending danger.

Early in the spring as the days were getting longer and they reached their hunting ground they saw a wolf approaching them from the direction of the camp where their enemies made their home. The wolf howled as it came closer and closer. Whenever it stopped, it barked at them. This was the manner in which the wolf came in their direction.

As the wolf got closer it was now plain to see that it was a wolf, so it started to veer off to their right. As the wolf got closer it looked in the direction of the attackers and started to bark in that direction. It was in this manner that the people started to suspect that they were being warned and at once they knew that people were coming to their direction with a hostile intent.

This was the working of ARNATTIAQ; she had sent this wolf to warn her relatives.

At this time the people tried not to move away too far from the iceberg where they had prepared for their refuge. Soon after the incident with the wolf, a dog team came into view.

Noah Piugaattuk, 1990.

Arctic Fox
Alopex lagopus

APPEARANCE

The Arctic fox has a round head, a blunt nose, short, rounded ears, and short legs. It is the only canid to change colours with the seasons. During the winter, its thick coat is white or bluish-grey. The bluish-grey fox is referred to as the blue fox. By early spring it begins to change colour. The back, tail and outer legs turn brown and the belly and sides become a yellowish-white. The summer coat is much shorter than the winter one. The Arctic fox looks much bigger than it actually is because of its incredibly thick fur. After the swift fox, the Arctic fox is the smallest wild canid in Canada, weighing between 2.5 and 5 kg. The adult female, or vixen, averages 82 cm in length and the adult male, an average of 89 cm. The long bushy tail is about half the length of its body.

Paul Nicklen

FOOD AND FEEDING

In the winter, the Arctic fox feeds mainly on lemmings and voles. It will also eat arctic hare and ptarmigan when available, as well as any leftovers from wolves, bears and humans. During the summer it adds eggs, ground squirrels, and fish to its diet. Scientists generally believe that the crash of lemming populations may cause Arctic fox populations to crash. Following a crash, the number of surviving fox pups declines. Many adults will starve the following winter and may not reproduce the next spring.

BEHAVIOUR

Arctic foxes live the life of nomads, travelling around in search of food. They live in dens that are dug in gentle slopes near rivers, lakes, or on higher ground free of permafrost. They have a well-developed system of tunnels with several entrances leading to their dens. Many dens are used for centuries, and they will often store some food in them and other places for later use. There can be as many as six occupied dens for every square kilometre. During the breeding season, they live in family groups made up of one male, a litter of pups, and a vixen. Otherwise, Arctic foxes usually live alone. When a group gets together to feed on leftovers from another animal, they often fight amongst themselves. They have a high-pitched bark and will hiss and scream, but not howl. They have a keen sense of smell and can detect lemmings in their nests under the snow. Arctic foxes are active all winter. At times, they will trail behind polar bears to *scavenge* food, and have ended up on some of the remotest Arctic islands by doing this. Although their home range varies between 16 and 25 square kilometres, they are capable of travelling far greater distances than the red fox. For example, some foxes from the Keewatin coast have ended up on Cornwallis Island.

Range

Canada

RANGE

Arctic foxes are found throughout Nunavut.

HABITAT

Arctic foxes are found mainly in Arctic and alpine tundra, coastal areas, and some forested areas in the southern portion of their range.

REPRODUCTION

Arctic foxes breed once a year between mid-February and April, depending on the physical health and geographic location of the animals. At this time, they often travel with a mate. In years of plenty they breed earlier, and in years of starvation they breed later, and sometimes not at all. The amount of food available also dictates the size of the litter. Arctic foxes can have between 4 and 25 pups at a time. The *gesta-*

Paul Nicklen

tion period is a little bit less than two months, and the pups are born between mid-May and mid-June, depending on geographic location. The young are born blind, deaf, and toothless, and weigh about 57 g each. They are born with a soft, velvety, dark brown undercoat that grows quickly and turns paler after a few weeks. The young pups come out of the den when they are between two and four weeks old and are *weaned* at about this time. They may be moved from one den to another by their parents and will be brought food for a short time before they are left on their own. The pups go their own way the following spring and reach sexual maturity at the age of 9 to 10 months.

STATUS, SURVIVAL AND MANAGEMENT

According to the Nunavut Wild Species 2000 report, the status of the Arctic fox is currently *secure*. The Arctic fox lives an average of four years, and predators in Nunavut include humans and other carnivores, and the young may be vulnerable to some birds. As the red fox continues to move farther north, it presents a source of competition to the Arctic fox for available food resources. Rabies and distemper are the most common diseases that affect the Arctic fox, and an outbreak can wipe out a large percentage of their population.

DID YOU
KNOW ?

Arctic fox, or *Alopex lagopus*, means "hare-footed fox." The name refers to t similarity between the thickly furred feet of a hare and an arctic fox. Also, t Arctic fox has something called "counter-current blood circulation." This mea the feet are always supplied with warm blood and therefore they stay just abo freezing temperature, even in extreme cold.

Pauli Kunnuk shares some memories of fox trapping.

The trappers that had their traps set close by had them set all over the place. They would only check some of their traps on the same day; otherwise the foxes would have been disturbed by the frequent activity and would move to other areas. They made sure to skip a day between checks to their traps. When I started to hunt on my own I no longer found it feasible to have my traps set nearby. When the trapping season opened one may have been able to trap foxes on a regular basis, but after the return of the sun in the wintertime, yields became poor for the traps that were set close by. So when I started trapping on my own, I preferred to go to distant places to trap where one had to spend days at a time checking out all the traps. I found that when we had our traps set at a distance, the yield would continue on a regular basis even when the days were getting longer and longer.

Pauli Kunnuk, 1990

Michel Kupaaq Piugaattuk shares information about fox trapping and method of payment for furs.

Before the leg hold traps were used, the people used to trap fox from Ullisautit so that they could trade the skins for lead for their firearms. They would go to the places where the white people had settled themselves.

In those days fox pelts were very often used for clothing. Most often, the fur was used for insulation. I once heard that the foxtail was big enough for an undershirt. The fox meat was also used, which I liked as well.

There were years when there were hardly any fox followed by years of plenty. When they were trapped as an article of trade it appeared as if they were never trapped to extinction but when they were no longer trapped, it seemed as if there were less. From the time of my childhood, I remember that they were highly sought after, as they were valued articles of trade. Something else I remember is that whenever there was an abundance of fox they would start to have rabies. It seems to be the same today as I have heard that this winter there is an abundance of fox and that they have started to have rabies.

Michel Kupaaq Piugaattuk, 1991

Red Fox

Vulpes vulpes

APPEARANCE

Red foxes are bigger than Arctic foxes. They have pointed faces and ears and long, bushy tails. Although they are called red foxes, there are three different *colour phases*. Foxes in the red phase are the most common and are reddish-brown with a white chest, abdomen, and tail tip. They have black hairs on their legs and down their backs. Foxes known as the cross fox are a grey-brown colour with black hairs across their shoulders, which form a cross. Lastly, there are silver foxes, which are black and have white tail tips and some silver highlights on their *guard hairs*. There can be all three phases in the same litter. Males are a little bigger than females. The average weight for males and females is between 3.6 and 6.8 kg. The total length is between 90 and 112 cm, and the tail can measure up to half this length.

Paul Nicklen

Paul Nicklen

FOOD AND FEEDING

The red fox is *omnivorous* and will eat whatever is available, depending on the seasons. Small mammals make up a large portion of the winter diet and include moles, shrews, muskrats, voles, and mice, as well as hares. During the summer, it will also feed on birds' eggs, some insects, and vegetation, such as grasses and berries. A red fox will eat almost anything, including seal pups, beaver, garbage, and carcasses left by other animals. One of the reasons the red fox is so widely distributed is that it can eat almost anything and therefore is less sensitive to population crashes in specific species. The red fox has keen senses and hunts by smell, sight, and sound. It may hear movement underground and dig until it locates the prey by using its excellent sense of smell.

BEHAVIOUR

Red foxes are shy and nervous animals that appear to be very intelligent and are most active at night. They have a high-pitched bark that is used when they are startled or to warn other foxes of danger. They run with a light, quick stride, leaving pawprints in a line in the snow. The family stays together from the time of mating until the pups go out on their own. For the rest of the year, during the autumn and winter, the animals live a solitary life. Red foxes live in dens usually located in sandy or gravelly soil, on small knolls, on riverbanks, or on the edge of a forest. They sometimes take over and fix up an abandoned den. The same dens may be used year after year, and they usually have more than one den for escape purposes.

Range
Nunavut
Canada

RANGE

The red fox is found throughout Canada and in many parts of Nunavut, including Baffin Island, Southampton Island, and most parts of Kitikmeot and Kivalliq Regions. It has been spotted as far north as Resolute Bay and on the southern coast of Ellesmere Island. It has adapted well to the Arctic tundra habitat and competes with the Arctic fox. The red fox has been known to travel as far as 250 km from where it was born, in search of a new home and food.

HABITAT

Red foxes live in places close to lakeshores, in river valleys, natural clearings, and in alpine and Arctic tundra. Normal home ranges vary between 5 and 35 square kilometres.

REPRODUCTION

The breeding period for red foxes is sometime between February and March, depending on geographic location. Many scientists believe that red foxes will stay as a pair for life, mating every year, sharing in the responsibilities of raising the pups, and then going their separate ways until they meet again the following year. The *gestation period* for red foxes is just under two months and the pups are born at different times during the spring, depending on geographic location. An average of five pups are born per litter. The pups weigh about 100 g at birth and are blind. Their eyes open during their second week of life, and they can be seen playing at the entrance to the den when they are a month old. By this time, the young foxes are able to eat small mammals brought to them by their parents but only if the parents chew them first. The pups leave and go out on their own when they are between 3.5 and 4 months old to find their own hunting territory. They reach sexual maturity at 10 months.

STATUS, SURVIVAL AND MANAGEMENT

According to the Nunavut Wild Species 2000 report, the current status of the red fox is *secure*. Few live longer than three or four years in the wild. The main predators for the red fox in Nunavut include humans and other carnivores, and the young may be vulnerable to some birds. It has been an important fur-bearing animal in the history of trapping in Canada. Demand and price have depended on the *colour phase* of the fox. The red phase has brought the lowest price, and the silver phase the highest. The price for the cross fox has landed somewhere in the middle. The red fox is one of the major carriers of both rabies and distemper. Because it travels such long distances, these diseases have quickly spread throughout the Arctic. Environmental health officers and local volunteers continue efforts to vaccinate foxes against rabies and distemper.

DID YOU KNOW ?

Red foxes traveled to the Arctic islands sometime in the 1940s. They adapted very well and have competed with Arctic foxes and other carnivores for food and shelter ever since.

Felidae

Lynx

Lynx canadensis

APPEARANCE

Lynx are easily identifiable by the thick collars of fur around their necks and pointy tufts of black fur on their ears. They have pale eyes and some small black stripes on their heads. Their fur is a grey-brown mixture, with paler brown on the belly, legs, and feet. In the late spring, their fur darkens to a reddish-brown. They are medium-sized animals that appear larger due to their thick coat of fur and long legs. Females are generally between 76 and 98 cm long and weigh between 5 and 12 kg. Males are generally between 76 and 108 cm long and weigh between 7 and 17 kg.

Paul Nicklen

FOOD AND FEEDING

Lynx are carnivores and will eat many different rodents, birds, fish, deer, and *carrion*. However, the snowshoe hare is their main food source, and changes in hare populations have a direct affect on the lynx populations.

BEHAVIOUR

Although they are excellent tree climbers, lynx are more often found on the ground, hunting for hares. They are most active during the night and periods of twilight. Their eyes are well adapted for seeing in low light, and they have excellent depth perception. Their sense of hearing is better than their sense of smell. They hunt by searching places where hares are most likely to live and chasing them out.

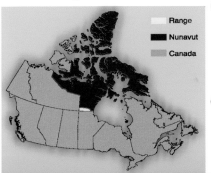

Range
Nunavut
Canada

RANGE

In Nunavut, the lynx can be found in southern Kivalliq Region, following the tree line.

HABITAT

The habitat for lynx is primarily forested areas, although it may range into the mountains, rocky areas, the tundra and the edge of the Arctic prairies.

DSD

REPRODUCTION

The breeding period for lynx is generally from mid-March to early April. After a *gestation period* of about two months, between one and five kittens are born. The kittens grow rapidly, and their first winter is spent learning to hunt with their mother. As spring approaches, the family group breaks up and the young look for their own range.

STATUS, SURVIVAL, AND MANAGEMENT

According to the Nunavut Wild Species 2000 report, the current status of lynx is *sensitive*. They can live up to 24 years in captivity. Their main predators in Nunavut include humans and wolves. They are harvested for their fur, and careful monitoring of the population is important so as not to overharvest when the populations are low following a crash in the snowshoe hare population.

DID YOU KNOW ?

The lynx has wide, furry paws that act like snowshoes and allow it to walk throug deep snow without problems.

Polar Bear
Ursus maritimus

APPEARANCE

Scientists believe that the polar bear *evolved* from the grizzly bear about two million years ago. It is the largest of all bears, but the polar bear's shape is quite different from the grizzly or black bear. Its body, especially the neck and the legs, are much longer than that of other bears, and it has a long head and small ears. The polar bear is completely covered with fur, with the exception of its nose and the pads of its feet. However, the areas between the pads on the feet are well furred. The polar bear's thick fur is made of a dense layer of under-hair covered by an outer layer of glossy *guard hairs*. The coat can vary from pure white to a creamy yellow, depending on the time of year and the angle of light. The males weigh between 350 and over 650 kg and females normally weigh between 150 and 250 kg, although this can double when they are pregnant.

Paul Nicklen

FOOD AND FEEDING

The polar bear's diet consists mainly of fat from seals and other marine mammals. They feed mainly on ringed seals but also hunt bearded, harp, and hooded seals, as well as young walrus. Sometimes, large males capture beluga whales. In addition, they may eat seabirds, eggs, and the carcasses of stranded marine mammals, fish, mussels, crabs, grasses, seaweed, mosses, and sedge if they come upon them, but they do not generally hunt or look for these foods.

BEHAVIOUR

Polar bears are skilled hunters. They use their powerful jaws and paws to capture seals and drag them out of the water. Their sharp *incisors* allow them to snip the fat away from the skin and meat. Whether they eat the whole seal or only the fat and some of the meat depends on the time of year and the overall health of the bear. In the spring, when females are emerging from their dens with their cubs, they usually consume the entire seal, with the exception of the skull, larger bones of the skeleton, and flippers. Single mature males, on the other hand, are more likely to feed on the fat of a seal, and leave the rest on the ice. Younger bears, as well as many other Arctic animals, benefit from the leftovers that an older bear has discarded. Polar bears are generally clean animals and will wash after they have finished feeding, either by rubbing their heads in the snow or swimming. They are well known for their excellent swimming ability. During their travels, they swim across bays and wide leads without trouble, and during the summer,

Paul Nicklen

they may spend hours in the water for no apparent reason. Unlike black bears and grizzly bears, polar bears do not hibernate. However, pregnant polar bears enter dens for about four months during the winter when they give birth to cubs. In addition, bears of all ages and both sexes may dig temporary dens for periods of up to several weeks to escape cold or stormy weather. If a polar bear does not feed for about 10 days, its body changes into a hibernation state, with a lowered *metabolism* and body temperature. This is similar to a black or brown bear, but the big difference is that polar bears can change into this state at any time of the year. As they are primarily meat-eaters and get their food from the sea, they are active throughout the winter, with the exception of pregnant females.

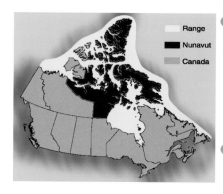

Range
Nunavut
Canada

RANGE

The polar bear can be found throughout Nunavut, mainly close to the coastline, but some animals may travel many kilometres inland to den or simply to cross islands and get to other hunting areas.

HABITAT

Polar bears can be found on the annual ice throughout the circumpolar Arctic. The seasons, availability of food and good denning sites, sea-ice conditions, and breeding season are all factors that affect where polar bears may be found. In Canada, they have been seen as far as 88° north and as far south as the Gulf of Saint Lawrence, although these are extremes and few bears actually reach those locations.

REPRODUCTION

Females generally begin to breed between three and five years of age. Males and females mate in the spring from April to June, depending on geographic location. After the bears mate, the fertilized egg remains undeveloped until mid-September to mid-October, after which it implants itself and begins to grow. The cubs are born two months later. The female will exca-

vate a den and enter sometime between late August and mid-November, depending on latitude and the area in general. In early January, the mother gives birth to a litter of cubs. Twins are most common, but often a single cub is born in first pregnancies. Litters of three and even four have been recorded. The cubs are about 40 cm long and weigh no more than 0.7 kg at birth. They are blind, deaf, and completely dependent on their mothers. The first few weeks following birth are spent in the den, feeding, sleeping, and gaining weight and strength. In some parts of Nunavut, cubs are ready to leave the den with their mother by mid-March or early April. For the first few days they stay around the den while the young get used to being outside. Shortly after, the cubs follow their mother and begin the journey to the sea-ice. The mother hunts and the cubs are nourished through her fatty milk. The young cubs have an immediate taste for seal and begin their hunting lessons during their first summer. Although they begin to eat fat and meat, they generally continue to nurse until they are almost two years old. A family group generally stays together until the third spring when the cubs are two and a halfs years old. The family breaks up and the female generally breed shortly thereafter.

STATUS, SURVIVAL AND MANAGEMENT

According to the Nunavut Wild Species 2000 report, the status of polar bears in Nunavut is currently *sensitive*. Polar bears live between 20 to 35 years in the wild and up to 40 years in captivity. Humans are their primary predator. Hunting regulations and *sustainable harvest-*

ing practices are continuing to be implemented in order to protect the bears. Polar bears are very sensitive to the *bio-accumulation* of pollutants in their bodies. This happens because pollutants like *PCBs* are attracted to fat and get deposited there. As each animal in the food chain eats the animal below it, the pollutants get passed on. As the species at the top of the food chain, polar bears accumulate all the pollutants from the other animals. Global warming has also had a direct effect on polar bears. Warmer winters mean shorter winters with less sea-ice. In places where the sea-ice melts completely during the summer, bears are finding themselves with longer periods on land as they wait for the ice to form. This could affect their overall health and reduce their chances of survival and reproduction, and may lower the survival rate of their cubs. Some of these effects are now being seen in western Hudson Bay. Polar bears need the sea-ice as a platform from which to hunt. As they wait for the ice to form, the chance of bears becoming a nuisance and a threat around communities also increases. Scientists are studying the polar bear in order to find out the extent that modern society has affected and will continue to affect their habitat and overall health.

DID YOU
KNOW ?

Bears have the incredible ability to absorb fat through their stomach lining. This means that soon after a bear eats seal fat, it seeps through the stomach lining and becomes part of its fat store. This is an extraordinary adaptation, as it allows the bear to accumulate a thick fat lining without using a lot of energy in the digestion process. Also, polar bears have black skin! A special layer of seal-like skin prevents them from getting puckered skin due to spending a lot of time in the water.

Paul Nicklen

Noah Piugaattuk shares some of his knowledge and stories about polar bears hunting seals.

I have seen polar bears hunting seals on more than one occassion. When the ice is hardly covered by snow, especially on older ice that has almost become land fast ice, the ice would be thicker than the younger ice. A polar bear goes to the aglu (breathing hole) and positions itself right next to it to wait for a seal to breathe. The aglu is covered with ice so it would be difficult to open it quickly. It would be unwise to open the cone-shaped ice built up over the aglu. So what he starts to do is claw his way through the ice right outside the nunataq. As he worked on the ice with his claws he made the hole quite large. The hollow that the bear has clawed through is in an angle so that it slants towards the direction of the breathing hole. Before his claws go right through the ice he will stop clawing when he reaches the ice that has not hardened in the freezing process. He will make the hole large, but will not dig any deeper once he reaches the soft ice. When he is satisfied that he can penetrate the ice that is facing the direction of the breathing hole and have a shot at the seal he takes his position and waits. When he takes his position he covers the hole he just made with his body so that no light goes through it. Unlike human hunters, he does not have anything that can make a ruffle to the ice so everything is quite as if the aglu was undisturbed. As soon as the seal comes up for air he will plunge through the hole he has just dug and it is in this manner that he can catch seals without using their natural breathing hole. I have seen this done on more than one occasion. Once the bear has made his catch he pulls it through the same hole and the natural breathing hole remains untouched. That is the way they hunt seal when all of the aglus are covered with ice.

Noah Piugaattuk, 1989

Barrenground Grizzly Bear
Ursus arctos

APPEARANCE

Grizzly bears are the second-largest carnivores after the polar bear. They have large heads with long *snouts* and two small, round, heavily furred ears. One of the ways to distinguish grizzly bears from black bears is that grizzlies have a noticeable hump on their shoulders.

The claws of the front feet are long, sharp, and pale yellow or brown in colour. Before shedding every year, grizzlies have long shaggy coats. Their fur is made up of coarse *guard hairs* and a thick coat of *under-fur*. Around the shoulders, the hairs are longer and form a ruff. Colours range from light gold to almost black, with the lightest bears most commonly found on the barren lands or tundra. Grizzly bears in Nunavut are generally smaller than those found farther south. Time of year plays a significant role in the bears' size. They are at their largest in the fall before entering their dens and leanest in the spring, when they emerge from their dens. Generally, females are smaller than males and reach their maximum weight before males do. Adult males and females can be anywhere between 146 and 382 kg and measure an average of 2.6 m in length.

DSD

FOOD AND FEEDING

Grizzlies are *omnivorous*. Some studies show that caribou are a very important food source for barrenground grizzlies. They appear to hunt them often during the spring, and from mid-summer to autumn. The caribou calving season comes at the same time as when the bears are emerging from their dens in the spring. The young caribou provide a great source of food for the hungry bears and newborns. In addition, they feed on many small mammals, such as lemmings, red-backed voles, ground squirrels, and also some birds, ringed seals, beached whales, and various kinds of spawning fish. During different times in the summer, horsetail, sedge, Arctic cotton grass, and various berries make up a large portion of the bears' diet.

BEHAVIOUR

Grizzly bears are generally solitary animals, although small groups may be seen feeding at the same area at certain times of the year. When this happens, the smaller bears give way to the larger bears. Grizzlies have good eyesight, but their hearing and sense of smell are excellent. They growl and roar when fighting and can run with great bursts of speed. These bears are most active in the evening, during the night, and at early morning. The area of their home range is largely dependent on the availability of food and the sex of the bear. Males tend to roam farther than females. In late summer the bears begin to fatten up and get ready to enter their dens for the winter months. Denning occurs in late October and November and may be weather dependent. Like black bears, their body temperatures drop slightly, and they fall into a deep slumber. However, they can be awakened by noise or disturbances in the area. The timing when grizzlies enter and emerge from their dens varies, depending on their geographic location.

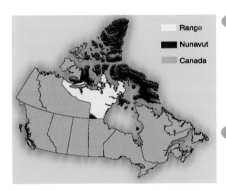

Range
Nunavut
Canada

RANGE

In Nunavut, the grizzly can be found throughout Kivalliq Region and in large portions of Kitikmeot and Baffin Regions.

HABITAT

Grizzlies live in various habitats but prefers *esker*, tall scrub- and lichen-rich habitats. They live in alpine tundra, high mountains, sub-alpine forests, alpine meadows, barren lands, and areas along coastlines.

REPRODUCTION

The breeding season for grizzlies differs with geographic location but is generally late spring to early summer. After a *gestation period* of six to eight months, including a period of *delayed implantation*, the female gives birth to usually two cubs, although one, three, and even four are also possible. They are born in mid-winter and are the size of a small squirrel, weighing between 350 and 700 g. They are blind, hairless, and helpless, but grow rapidly. Grizzlies have a litter every third year and the young stay with the mother for two and possibly three years. In Nunavut, female grizzlies usually have their first litter at eight years of age. Compared to other grizzly populations, this is quite late, and makes barren ground grizzlies more sensitive to overharvesting.

STATUS, SURVIVAL, AND MANAGEMENT

According to the Nunavut Wild Species 2000 report, the status of grizzly bears is *sensitive*. Grizzlies live up to 25 years in the wild and possibly up to 50 in captivity. They have no natural enemies other than humans. An increase in the number of encounters between humans and grizzlies is resulting in more "nuisance" bears being killed. Hunting regulations and bear safety programs continue to be enforced in an effort to protect the slow-growing populations.

DSD

DID YOU KNOW ?

Not all scientists agree that grizzly bears truly hibernate. The disagreement is based on the fact that the grizzlies' body temperature does not drop significantly, as it does in other species. They prefer to call what grizzlies experience a period of dormancy.

Black Bear
Ursus americanis

APPEARANCE

Black bears are not always black. They range in colour from blonde to brown to black. The most common colour in Nunavut is black, with a tan *muzzle* and a cream V-shape on the chest. Black bears have large heads and short necks. Their eyes are small and black, their ears are rounded, and their *snouts* are long. Black bears vary in size a great deal during the year and are heaviest in the autumn and leanest in the spring. Generally, females weigh between 90 and 110 kg and males between 115 and 170 kg. Both are usually between 1.5 and 1.8 m long and almost 1 m high at the shoulder.

Paul Nicklen

FOOD AND FEEDING

Black bears eat a wide variety of food, and this makes it possible for them to adapt to many environments. They feed on berries, fruits, nuts, twigs, leaves, roots, insects, larvae, eggs, *carrion*, honey, and small mammals. Unfortunately, in some places bears have gotten used to eating garbage produced by humans, and looking for food in the wild then becomes secondary.

BEHAVIOUR

Black bears are generally solitary, although a gathering of several bears may occur in places that have an abundance of food. They have poor eyesight, but their sense of smell and hearing are excellent. They can run quickly and swim short distances. Black bears hibernate during the winter, and in Nunavut they will begin seeking out denning sites in September. During hibernation, the bear's body temperature drops about five degrees and their *metabolism* is slightly lower than usual. They do not eat or expel fluids or wastes during this time. When they emerge from their dens in the spring, they are lean and looking for food.

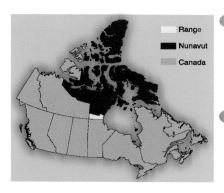

Range
Nunavut
Canada

RANGE

The range of the black bear in Nunavut is limited to the southern part of Kivalliq Region, following the tree line.

HABITAT

The black bear's main habitat is forested areas, but it can also be found in swamps, marshes, and thickets, and on the tundra.

REPRODUCTION

The breeding season for the black bear can begin as early as May and last until August. Mating is competitive, and males may fight aggressively for the right to mate with a female. After a *gestation period* of seven to seven and a half months, including a period of *delayed implantation*, one to four cubs are born. The cubs weigh between 240 and 330 g at birth and are blind, hairless and helpless. At six months, the cubs may weigh up to 25 kg, and although they are independent, they usually spend the winter with their mother and go off on their own or with a sibling the following spring. Females generally mate every two years.

STATUS, SURVIVAL, AND MANAGEMENT

According to the Nunavut Wild Species 2000 report, the current status of the black bear in Nunavut is *not assessed*. Although black bears can live for 25 to 30 years in the wild, they usually survive for less than 10 years. Black bears' main predators in Nunavut include humans and other carnivores.

DID YOU KNOW ?

Black bears may look like they move awkwardly, but they are capable of great bursts of speed when they need it. For short distances, they have been clocked at speeds of 55 km/h!

Wolverine
Gulo gulo

APPEARANCE

The wolverine is one of the larger species in the weasel family. It has a wide, broad head, short, rounded ears, small, black, beady eyes, and a black *muzzle*. It has a solid, muscular body, a short, bushy tail, and strong legs. Its large bear-like paws have five strong, partly retractable claws. The wolverine has long, coarse fur, including a dense layer of *under-fur*. Generally, it is a rich, glossy, dark brown and may have some speckled grey on the forehead and tips of the ears. There are some cream spots on the chest, back, and throat. The soles of the feet are furred. Females are smaller than males, usually measuring 90 cm long and weighing 10.5kg. Males are generally one metre long and weigh 15 kg.

Paul Nicklen

BEHAVIOUR

The wolverine is popularly thought to be able to stand up to grizzly bears and outsmart humans by evading their traps and raiding their *caches* of food. Perhaps some of the stories are exaggerated, but it is truly a remarkable mammal. It is curious, bold and strong. A wolverine will defend its food from many animals much larger than itself. It has well-developed scent glands and marks its territory as well as its food to discourage others from taking it. The wolverine is a solitary animal and does not generally allow a wolverine of the same sex to enter its territory. It has a keen sense of smell, but appears to have poor eyesight. The wolverine is active both day and night and can travel great distances in search of food without tiring. It follows migrating caribou herds and cleans up the carcasses left by wolves and bears. If cornered, a wolverine will growl, bark, and hiss.

FOOD AND FEEDING

The wolverine is *omnivorous* and primarily a *scavenger*. Although it has the strength to kill large game animals, such as deer, caribou, and moose, it only does this occasionally. The wolverine travels long distances to scavenge for food rather than kill it. In addition to feeding on *carrion* and big game animals in the winter, it eats eggs from ground-nesting birds, edible roots, and berries during the summer months.

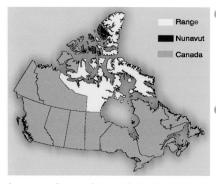

Range
Nunavut
Canada

RANGE

In Nunavut, the wolverine can be found in all regions, except on parts of the highest Arctic islands.

HABITAT

Formerly, wolverines inhabited the boreal forests of North America. Today, they are more likely to be found on the tundra between the tree line and the Arctic coasts. They can also be found among rocky outcrops and on steep canyon sides or open plains.

REPRODUCTION

The breeding season is between late April and early September. After a *gestation period* of six to eight months, including a period of *delayed implantation*, between two and five young are born. In Nunavut, the kits are generally born in late March and early April. Newborn wolverines have a fuzzy, creamy-white fur coat, paws, and a facemask. During the early summer,

Paul Nicklen

the cubs stay in the den and the mother brings them food. As they get older, they follow her and she teaches them to hunt. The cubs stay with the mother during their first winter and leave in the spring. Females have one litter every two or three years.

STATUS, SURVIVAL, AND MANAGEMENT

According to the Nunavut Wild Species 2000 report, the current status of wolverine is *sensitive*. Wolverines can live several years in the wild and up to 17 years in captivity. In Nunavut, their predators include humans, and occasionally wolf packs or bears. A long-term monitoring program of the harvested wolverine population has been going on in western Kitikmeot Region since 1985–86 and is now extended to the east of Kitikmeot and Kivalliq Regions.

Wolverines do not have many predators; however, porcupines have indirectly killed some! This may happen when a wolverine eats a porcupine and some quills are not digested properly. The quills may pierce its stomach and lead to internal bleeding and death.

Ermine
Mustela erminea

APPEARANCE

The ermine is a small, lean, ferocious carnivore. Its ears are short, round, and covered with a thin layer of fur. The head is long, narrow, and flat. It has two very different *colour phases*. The summer phase includes a brown head and back, while the belly and the undersides of the legs and toes are white. The tail is brown with a black tip. During the winter, the ermine is completely white, except for a black-tipped tail and some yellowish colouring around the rump from the discharge of the scent glands. The change of colour is brought on by the changing light in the spring and autumn. Males are about twice as large as females. The average adult male is usually 35 cm in length and weighs an average of 80 g. The average length of an adult female is generally 29 cm and the average weight is 54 g. The tail makes up about one-third of the total body length.

Paul Nicklen

FOOD AND FEEDING

Ermine hunt and kill mice, ground squirrels, chipmunks, lemmings, and shrews. They also feed on hares, porcupines, birds, fish, beavers, and pocket gophers where available. Ermine are generally believed to kill much more than they can possibly eat. This is not true. Although they do kill many animals, they stash these in their dens to make sure they have a steady supply of food. Ermine, like other species in the mustelid family, have a very high *metabolism*, and because of this, they must eat often. The small size of their stomachs is another challenge for the ermine, as this means they can only eat a small amount of food at a time.

BEHAVIOUR

Ermine are confident and daring hunters. Their slight builds allow them to move around quickly and enter small openings that lead into burrows and nests. They are efficient hunters, grabbing the shoulder area of their prey and biting through the neck at the base of the skull. If the prey is large, they may be swept off their feet and swung sideways, but will hang on with their jaws until the animal tires and dies. The ermine has three different ways of vocalizing: a trill, a screech, and a squeal. The trill is used to communicate with others, especially between a mother and her young. The screech is used to frighten prey, and the squeal is usually an expression of pain or trouble.

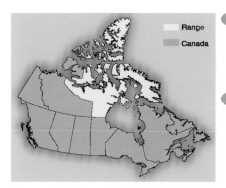

Range
Canada

RANGE

The ermine can be found throughout Nunavut.

HABITAT

Ermine have a wide range of habitat. They can be found in boreal and mixed forests, on the tundra, and along meadows, riverbanks, and lakeshores. They can live at sea level or at an altitude of more than 3,000 m above sea level.

REPRODUCTION

The *gestation period* for ermine is 10 months, including a period of *delayed implantation*. They mate in the early spring or summer, but implantation does not occur until the following March. Once implantation occurs, they give birth about one month later. The average litter size is 6, but there can be up to 10 young. The young ermine are covered with a thin layer of white fur at birth, and their eyes and ears are shut. After about three weeks they have a good fur coat, and after five weeks their eyes open and they may travel close to their mother. By seven weeks, the males are as big as their mother. Although males grow rapidly, they will not reach sexual maturity until the following spring. The female, on the other hand, reaches sexual maturity at two to three months of age and is ready to reproduce each spring.

STATUS, SURVIVAL, AND MANAGEMENT

According to the Nunavut Wild Species 2000 report, the current status for ermine in Nunavut is *secure*. They live up to seven years in the wild. Their main predators are carnivores and birds.

DID YOU
KNOW ?

Ermine fur was used in making outfits for royalty and as decoration on much aboriginal clothing.

APPEARANCE

The least weasel is the smallest carnivore in North America. It has a small head with short, oval ears, black, beady eyes, and a pointy nose. Its body is long and slender, and it has two *colour phases*. During the summer, the least weasel has brown fur on its back, white on its belly, and whitish feet with furred soles. In the winter, it is completely white and may have a few black hairs on the tip of its tail. The female is usually 16 to 18 cm in length and weighs 25 to 57 g. The male is generally 18 to 22 cm in length and weighs 34 to 62 g.

FOOD AND FEEDING

The least weasel feeds mostly on small mammals and will occasionally eat insects.

BEHAVIOUR

Paul Nicklen

Least weasels take over the burrows of the small mammals they hunt and line their nests with the fur from their prey. At times, this fur can be up to 2.5 cm thick. They use it to keep themselves warm, and at times to thaw their dinners. Like some of the other species in this family, the least weasel keeps a *cache* of available food on hand. They have a high *metabolism* and eat about half their body weight each day. They seem to be clean animals and have a separate toilet area in their burrows. The least weasel is very agile and not often seen. It has a high, shrill shriek.

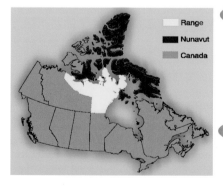

Range	(white)
Nunavut	(black)
Canada	(grey)

RANGE

In Nunavut, the least weasel can be found throughout Kivalliq Region, in southwestern Kitikmeot Region, and as in the western portion of Baffin Region on Melville Peninsula.

HABITAT

The least weasel can be found in fields, meadows, riverbanks, parklands, mixed forests, and tundra.

REPRODUCTION

Least weasels breed from February until mid-November. There is no period of *delayed implantation*, and females give birth after a *gestation period* of just over a month. There are 3 to 10 young per litter, and they can have two or more litters a year. The young are born blind and helpless, but develop rapidly and are *weaned* after four weeks. Males are not involved in raising the young. Females reach maturity at four months of age and males at eight months.

STATUS, SURVIVAL, AND MANAGEMENT

According to the Nunavut Wild Species 2000 report, the current status of the least weasel in Nunavut is *not assessed*. The least weasel can live up to about one year. Its main predators in Nunavut include other carnivores and some birds. The least weasel helps keep mouse and vole populations in check, but is not considered valuable as a fur-bearing animal.

DID YOU KNOW ?

The least weasel hunts by scent and pounces onto its victim's back, then bites into the skull with its small *canine* teeth.

George Kappianaq speaks about the different uses of amulets.

Little boys were sometimes given pigusiq. Pigusiq are rituals of placing amulets on a newborn so they would have special powers that were not available to ordinary people. In most cases amulets were used for this practise; things like the shape of a knife, the foot of a lemming, the foot of a weasel, or a fang. These were the things that would help boys in their adulthood. Some wore a weasel skin in the tip of their hood, kukukpaaq or hanging from the back flaps of their upper wear. These weasel skins would be able to assist them in times of hardship if they had nothing else to depend on in their adulthood while hunting, or if someone had in mind to murder them out of animosity. These skins enabled them to know about these things and others during times that they really needed help..

George Kappianaq, 1997

Mink
Mustela vison

APPEARANCE

The mink is a long, lean animal much like the ermine, with a pointed face, small ears, a long neck, and short legs. It is perhaps most popularly known for its thick, brownish-black, oily fur coat that protects and insulates it from the cold northern waters. Mink have been sought after by fur-trappers for centuries. As with the ermine, it has anal glands that give off a strong musky odour. Females are smaller than males and are generally 66 cm long and weigh an average of one kilogram. Males are generally 70 cm long and weigh an average of two kilograms. Its bushy tail is about half the size of its body.

Paul Nicklen

FOOD AND FEEDING

The mink's diet is made up of many different animals, as well as some vegetation. Mink hunt and consume many small mammals, such as voles, shrews, muskrats, and rabbits. As well, they consume some small fish, frogs, salamanders, and crayfish. They may occasionally eat insects, birds, and worms but these things make up a very small portion of their diet.

BEHAVIOUR

Mink are excellent swimmers and ferocious hunters. They live alone, with the exception of the mating season. *Juveniles* are playful and carefree but grow quickly into adulthood. Mink make a few different noises, ranging from soft murmurings during the mating season to high-pitched screeches and hissing when they are fighting. They do not travel great distances, usually staying close to rivers and often making their home in or around the riverbank.

Mink

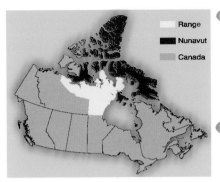

Range
Nunavut
Canada

RANGE

In Nunavut, mink can be found in the southern part of Kivalliq Region and the southwestern portion of Kitikmeot Region.

HABITAT

Mink often take over an abandoned muskrat or beaver home. They can be found around various kinds of freshwater sources, such as swamps, lakes, rivers, and streams. During the winter, when river and lake levels drop below the ice level, there is usually a small pocket of air between the two. This allows the mink to travel underneath the ice.

REPRODUCTION

Mink reproduce in the spring and have different lengths of *delayed implantation*, depending on how early or late in the season they mate. The female has one litter per year and can have between 2 and 10 young. The young mink are born blind, deaf, and with a light coating of fine white hair. They open their eyes and develop hearing at about five weeks of age. As they mature, they follow their mother on her hunting expeditions, and by the autumn they go off on their own. Males do not help raise the young. A female mink is sexually mature at 12 months and a male mink at 18 months.

STATUS, SURVIVAL, AND MANAGEMENT

According to the Nunavut Wild Species 2000 report, the current status of mink in Nunavut is *not assessed*. They live up to three or four years in the wild. In captivity, mink may live up to 10 years. Their main predators in Nunavut include other carnivores and humans.

DID YOU KNOW ?

Mink have partially webbed feet that help make them excellent swimmers!

Marten
Martes americana

Paul Nicklen

APPEARANCE

The marten has a broad head with a pointed nose, large ears, and big, black, beady eyes. Its body is slender and long, and its bushy tail is about half its length. The colour of its long silky coat varies in colour from pale beige to reddish and dark brown. The marten has short legs with *semi-retractable* claws. The female is smaller than the male and is generally 50 to 60 cm long and weighs between 590 and 770 g. Males are usually 55 to 65 cm long and weigh between 680 and 1,315 g.

FOOD AND FEEDING

The marten feeds mostly on rodents and other small mammals, especially voles. It also eats birds, insects, fruits, leftovers from other animals, and some fish.

BEHAVIOUR

Martens are mostly solitary, *nocturnal* animals. They are very curious animals and are always looking for food, which makes them very easy to trap. They spend a lot of time both in trees and on the ground hunting for food. They are active all winter and make their homes in trees or hollows among rocks. They usually have a permanent home range and stay within it. However, if the supply of food is low, they will spread out beyond their normal home range.

RANGE

In Nunavut, the marten can be found in southern Kivalliq Region and in the southwestern portion of Kitikmeot Region, following the tree line.

HABITAT

The marten can be found in conifer forests as well as in cedar swamps, in cutovers,

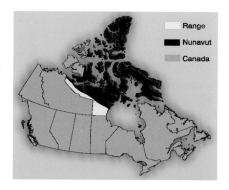

Range
Nunavut
Canada

around logging camps, and close to human settlements.

REPRODUCTION

The breeding season for martens is in July and August. The *gestation period* is between seven and nine months, including a lengthy period of *delayed implantation*. Between one and five young are born blind, helpless and covered with a thin coat of yellowish fur. Maturity is reached at 15 to 24 months.

STATUS, SURVIVAL, AND MANAGEMENT

According to the Nunavut Wild Species 2000 report, the current status of martens in Nunavut is *not assessed*. They can live up to five or six years in the wild and 18 years in captivity. Their main predators in Nunavut include other carnivores and humans.

DID YOU KNOW ?

Martens eat yellow-jacket hornets in the autumn.

Fisher
Martes pennanti

APPEARANCE

The fisher has a broad head, short, rounded ears, small eyes, and large feet with narrow, curved claws. Its thick, glossy coat ranges in colour from black to shades of brown, with some light-coloured hairs around the face and shoulders during the winter. Females are generally smaller than males, measuring 75 to 95 cm long and weighing between one and three kilograms. Males are usually 85 to 107c m in length and weigh between 2.5 and 5 kg.

FOOD AND FEEDING

Paul Nicklen

The fisher is popular, as it is one of the only mammals capable of hunting and eating porcupines. It generally eats anything it can overpower, and this includes its main prey, the hare, as well as small rodents, birds, fish, insects, and leftovers from other animals. Fishers also eat some plant material, like fruits, seeds, berries, and fern tips where available.

BEHAVIOUR

Fishers are generally solitary animals, somewhat secretive and hard to observe. They are keen hunters and travel along regular hunting circuits, using temporary dens while on the trail. They can be active during day or night and also stay active throughout the winter, except during severe weather, when they may wait out a storm in a temporary shelter. They prefer to walk on fallen logs and are good swimmers.

RANGE

Fishers are found in the southern portion of Kivalliq Region in Nunavut, following the tree line.

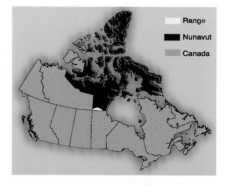

Range
Nunavut
Canada

HABITAT

Fishers generally live in well-forested areas with a good overhead *canopy*. This helps them avoid deep snow and is also a good place to find snowshoe hares.

REPRODUCTION

Fishers breed between March and April. After a *gestation period* of between 11 and 12 months, including a period of *delayed implantation*, one to four young are born in March and April of the following year. They are born helpless and stay with the mother for three to four months before going out on their own. Females reach maturity at one year and males at two years.

STATUS, SURVIVAL, AND MANAGEMENT

According to the Nunavut Wild Species 2000 report, the current status of the fisher in Nunavut is *not assessed*. Fishers live a maximum of 10 years in the wild. Their main predators in Nunavut include humans and possibly wolves.

DID YOU KNOW ?

The fisher kills a porcupine by biting its head repeatedly, flipping it on its back and eating through the stomach area. This is done while avoiding the quills on the porcupine's tail and back.

River Otter
Lutra lutra

APPEARANCE

The river otter spends most of its life in and around freshwater sources. It has a flat head and a thick, muscular neck. The river otter has a short, oily coat of thick *under-fur*, covered by a coat of rich brown *guard hairs*. There may be some silvery-grey fur on its throat. It has short legs and completely webbed feet. A female otter generally weighs between 4.5 and 11 kg and is between 88 and 116 cm long. A male usually weighs between 7 and 14 kg and is between 94 and 137 cm long.

FOOD AND FEEDING

Eyewire

The river otter feeds mostly on fish such as minnows, sunfish, sculpins, catfish, perch, and trout. It also eats floating birds, swimming up under them and pulling them underwater. Some of the small mammals it feeds on include shrews, meadow voles, muskrats, and young beavers.

BEHAVIOUR

Otters are mostly *nocturnal*, but may be seen in the early morning or late afternoon in some areas. They are active all winter; however, they may seek shelter for a few days to wait out severe weather. River otters do not dig their own dens; instead, they take over muskrat or beaver dens and make beds using pieces of dried grass, bark, and other dry vegetation. Otters have very keen senses and are excellent swimmers. They make a variety of noises, but the most usual is a sharp whistle. They also make chuckling and grunting noises. Otters are very playful and social, and this makes them very easy to train in captivity. They form a strong family bond and although the father leaves soon after the young are born, he may return when they are a few months old and help to raise them.

Paul Nicklen

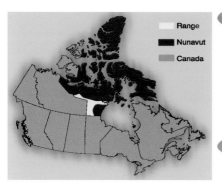

RANGE

In Nunavut, river otters are found in southern Kivalliq Region. They are limited to the North American continent, although there is a species similar in appearance in parts of Europe.

HABITAT

Otters can travel up to 100 km a year, but usually a range of 5 to 16 km along a stream bank is enough for one family. Most of their time is spent around the shores of lakes, rivers, streams, and marshes including rivers and lakes in the tundra, north of the tree line.

REPRODUCTION

The mating season for otters is late winter or early spring, soon after the birth of the young. The *gestation period* is between 9.5 and 12.5 months, including a period of *delayed implantation.* The litter size is between one and six, but is usually about two or three. At birth, the young are blind, have fur, and weigh about 132 g and measure about 27 cm in length. Play begins soon after their eyes open at five to six weeks of age. At about 10 to 12 weeks of age, the young start to explore the area outside the den with their mother. She teaches them to hunt and swim. The father joins the family when the young are about six months old. Sexual maturity is reached at about two years of age; however, males usually are not successful in mating until they are six or seven years old.

STATUS, SURVIVAL AND MANAGEMENT

According to the Nunavut Wild Species 2000 report, the status of river otters is *not assessed.* River otters live up to 13 years in the wild and between 14 and 20 years in captivity. The otters' main predators in Nunavut include some carnivores, and the young may be vulnerable to some birds. Historically, river otters have been sought after for their fur.

DID YOU KNOW ?

The river otter is very intelligent and easily tamed. In ancient times, they were often trained to catch fish for people!

Lagomorpha

Leporidae

Arctic Hare
Lepus arcticus

Paul Nicklen

APPEARANCE

Arctic hare are the most northern-dwelling of all hares, and are also among the largest. In the winter, their coats are long, white, and silky, and their ears are tipped with black. The summer coat ranges in colour through shades of grey, cinnamon-brown, and even a pinkish hue, depending on geographic location. Arctic hare have medium-sized ears and big, padded feet. The fur on their feet is a yellowish colour and they have long, curved claws, especially on their front feet. These are very useful for digging in the hard-packed snow. Females are between 60 and 70 cm long and males are between 60 and 80 cm in length. Males and females weigh between 2.5 and 5.4 kg.

FOOD AND FEEDING

Arctic hare eat a variety of tundra vegetation, including twigs and the roots of Arctic willow and crowberry. In addition, they may at times venture out onto the sea-ice in search of seaweed. Finally, Arctic hare also feed on meat, and are often attracted to bait left in traps.

BEHAVIOUR

Arctic hare do not appear to be very nervous around humans. However, if a dog, wolf, or fox approaches, the hare immediately bolt. They easily hide behind rocks, and unless a noise is very loud and close, they will not move. They have two ways of running: the more southern-dwelling hare run using all four legs, and the more northern-dwelling hare hop like a kangaroo, on their hind legs. They resume a four-legged run when danger has passed. At times, they hop up and down on their hind legs in an effort to scan the horizon for predators. Arctic hare either live alone or in family groups. Some are playful and have been observed "boxing" one another and standing on their hind legs dancing around. They are mainly *nocturnal*, but are also active in periods of twilight and just before sunrise. They are active all year long and sometimes huddle together to stay warm. They live in dens that have an entrance, which is about 10 cm in *diameter* and 30 cm long, with a larger diameter inside the den.

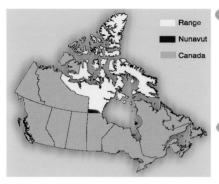

Range
Nunavut
Canada

RANGE

Arctic hare are found throughout Nunavut. Their home range is small, which allows them to build up a series of runways and escape routes.

HABITAT

Arctic hare are generally only found on the tundra beyond the tree line. In the winter, they tend to inhabit the northern slopes of hills, where the wind keeps the ground more exposed. They are only likely to be found on low plains during the summer.

REPRODUCTION

The breeding period is during the bright days of April and May. Arctic hare have a *gestation period* of about 50 days. They have one litter a year, with between two and eight young per litter. The young are born in a small depression in the moss or grass that may be protected by a boulder. Young hare are born with a full coat of grey fur and huddle together for warmth. Their weight, soon after birth is about 105 g and they measure about 17.5 cm. By early September they are fully grown, and they reach maturity at one year.

Paul Nicklen

STATUS, SURVIVAL AND MANAGEMENT

According to the Nunavut Wild Species 2000 report, the current status of arctic hare is *secure*. They are thought to live about five years. Their main predators in Nunavut include some carnivores and birds.

Young Arctic hare grow twice as fast as other species of hare due to short Arctic summers.

Alain Ijjiraq shares some memories about how the environment affects rabbit populations.

There used to be plenty of rabbits around until one year, the rain fell just before Christmas and froze over the snow, wiping out the rabbit population completely. It was only many years later that the population increased again. I remember the time; I guess when you had started to live in that area, I used to go out rabbit hunting at Avvajjaq and there used to be some tracks then, but now there are hardly any more tracks. I believe a lot of rabbits disappeared at the time it rained in the wintertime. It was the time I spent the winter at Qikirtaaluk. I moved there in November and did not return until April; it was at that time that the rabbit population was wiped out after the rain. I too used to enjoy eating rabbits.

Alain Ijjiraq, 1990.

Elise Qulaut shares a humorous story about the noise rabbits make.

Late in the autumn, we moved to the direction of our home. As we made our way home, the ground was covered in snow and there were a lot of rabbits. The three of us started to go out to hunt for rabbits and my brother shot at one. All at once the rabbit started to make a loud "ungaa" sound. I was so scared that I started to cry and both of us started to run for home. As it turned out, rabbits make loud sounds.

Elise Qulaut, 1990

Snowshoe Hare

Lepus americanus

APPEARANCE

Snowshoe hare have two main *colour phases*. In the winter they are completely white except for black-tipped ears, and during the summer months they turn a rusty-brown colour. Decreasing levels of daylight trigger their change of colour in the autumn, and increasing levels trigger the change in the spring. Snowshoe hare get their name from their padded, broad hind feet, which have thick, coarse hair and act as snowshoes. This allows the hare to move around easily, even in deep snow conditions. The snowshoe hare's weight changes during the season, peaking in December and June. Females may weigh a bit more than males. The average weight in November is about 1.5 kg for females and 1.45 kg for males. The total length for both is between 36 and 52 cm.

Hans-L Blohm

FOOD AND FEEDING

During the summer, the snowshoe hare feeds on tender vegetation like clovers, grasses, sedges, ferns, and *forbs*. In the winter, it eats buds, twigs, and the bark and evergreen leaves of woody plants. In addition, it may eat frozen meat and display *cannibalistic behaviour*.

BEHAVIOUR

The snowshoe hare's behaviour is similar to other species in its family. It is mainly *nocturnal* and remains active all winter. However, it may be seen on cloudy winter afternoons when the light intensity is not high. In addition, it may also be active during twilight and sunset. Although it takes long naps and spends a lot of time grooming itself, the snowshoe hare is always alert and ready to bolt in the event of danger. When young, it may rely more on its ability to "freeze" and blend into its surroundings in order to escape from predators, but adults prefer to bolt, as they can bound up to about three metres and travel as fast as 43 km/h. The snowshoe hare is a social animal, and many may inhabit the same area.

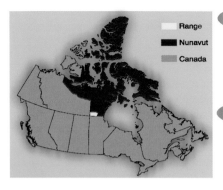

Range
Nunavut
Canada

RANGE

The snowshoe hare is found in a small portion of southern Kivalliq Region, within the tree line.

HABITAT

Ideally, the snowshoe hare dwells in dense second-growth forests, thickets, and swamps.

REPRODUCTION

The breeding season usually begins in March and ends in September, but is largely dependent on geographic location and season. After a *gestation period* of just over one month, one to eight young are born. There may be as many as four litters a year. The young are born with a silky fur coat, and their eyes open shortly after birth. Although they weigh only 65 to 80 g at birth, they gain weight rapidly and hop away from the nest after the sixth day. The young reach maturity the spring after their birth.

STATUS, SURVIVAL AND MANAGEMENT

According to the Nunavut Wild Species 2000 report, the status of snowshoe hares is *sensitive*. They live between three and five years in the wild. Their main predators in Nunavut include some carnivores and birds.

DID YOU KNOW ?

Snowshoe hares sometimes swim across rivers or small lakes. They float high in the water and propel themselves with their huge hind feet.

Patrick J. Endres/AlaksaPhotoGraphics

Rodentia

Castoridae
Muridae
Sciuridae

Beaver
Castor canadensis

APPEARANCE

The beaver is the national emblem of Canada. It has a rich, glossy brown or yellowish coat, with chestnut-brown to tawny underparts. The beaver's unique tail is well furred at the thick base, but it has only a little bit of hair on the flattened paddle. The skull of the beaver is large and sturdy so that it can support the strong muscles that are needed to cut down and drag trees through water and over land. The average size of an adult female from nose to tip of tail is 1.3 m. The average size of an adult male is 1.8 m in length. Weight for both is largely dependent on age, sex, and the season, and can be anywhere between 15 and 35 kg.

Paul Nicklen

FOOD AND FEEDING

The beaver is *herbivorous* and feeds on a variety of trees, leaves, and bark, as well as plants, depending on the season and availability.

BEHAVIOUR

Beavers have a well-developed social structure, and much could be written about their behaviour and habits. The family is the basic unit. Everybody in the family unit works together in building and maintaining the family home. The home may be in a bank burrow with an underwater access tunnel, or a lodge made of mud and tree branches. Beavers communicate by leaving scented mud-pies, by uttering a series of low whines, or by slapping their tail on the water as a warning to other beavers. They are most active between sunset and sunrise. Beavers do not hibernate; they stay active all winter underneath the ice, feeding on stored food and maintaining their homes.

HABITAT

Beavers inhabit lakes, slow-moving rivers, streams, and marshes. They are usually found in forested areas, but are occasionally found around prairie streams, muskeg, alpine meadows, and tundra. Aspen groves are their favourite habitat, but they can survive where shrub willows, alders, or water plants are their main source of food. Other than humans, beavers are the only animals that can change their environment. They do this by building dams and this results in the creation of very different habitats.

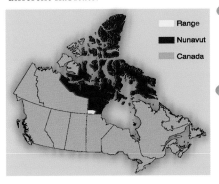

Range
Nunavut
Canada

RANGE

In Nunavut, the beaver is found in southern Kivalliq Region.

REPRODUCTION

Mating takes place in January and February, under the ice. The *gestation period* is about three and a half months, and the young are born between April and late June. Females can have anywhere between one and eight young each year, but can only nurse four. The young are born fully furred with slightly flattened tails, and are able to eat solid food as well as nurse from their mother. This ensures that if the mother has more young than she can nurse at once, they are able to survive. Young beavers measure about 125 mm and weigh about 450 g. They mature sexually during their second winter, but do not mate until their third or fourth winter.

STATUS, SURVIVAL, AND MANAGEMENT

According to the Nunavut Wild Species 2000 report, the current status if the beaver is *not assessed*. The beaver lives for 10 to 15 years in the wild and up to 24 years in captivity. Predators in Nunavut include some carnivores and birds. Historically, the beaver was responsible for the exploration and settlement of much of Canada, and has therefore been the most important economic trapping resource in Canada.

DID YOU KNOW ?

The beaver has valves to keep water from entering its nose and ears and a thin *membrane* that protects its eyes, allowing it to keep them open under water. The beaver has furry lips that close behind its teeth, allowing it to gnaw at wood underwater without swallowing any.

Muskrat
Ondatra zibethicus

APPEARANCE

The muskrat resembles the beaver in many ways, but is not a close relative. Some people think it is a rat, but it is more like a big field mouse that has adapted to living in and around water. It has a thick, waterproof coat made up of soft *under-fur* and long, coarse, shiny *guard hairs*. Its fur varies from a silvery brown to dark brown with grey underparts. It has a long, scaly, black tail, partially webbed toes, strong claws, and big hind feet that are slightly rotated. The average length and weight for a male and female is 56 cm and one kilogram.

Paul Nicklen

FOOD AND FEEDING

The muskrat feeds mostly on aquatic vegetation, and the cattail is one of its most important foods. It may also occasionally eat clams, mussels, and other small, water-dwelling organisms when available.

BEHAVIOUR

Muskrats live in family units around water. They can stay submerged for up to 17 minutes in times of stress, but the usual time is 2–3 minutes. The lack of fur on their feet and tail brings them out of the water to feed in order to conserve body heat. Where solid banks are available, muskrats build a burrow with an underwater entrance that connects to a nesting chamber. Where a solid bank isn't available, muskrats build lodges or pushups that rise about three feet above the water. When the surface of the water freezes, these pushups give them access to the food under the ice during the winter. Caribou will sometimes paw at these domes to eat the vegetation used to make them.

HABITAT

Muskrats generally live around a source of water that is deep enough that it will not freeze completely. Ponds, lakes, streams, canals, and reservoirs, and also freshwater marshes, are likely habitats for muskrats.

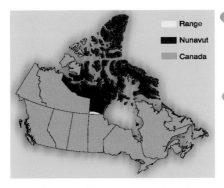

Range
Nunavut
Canada

RANGE

The muskrat can be found in southern Kivalliq Region.

REPRODUCTION

Breeding takes place between March and September, depending on geographic location. There are often vicious fights among muskrats during the breeding period; most adults are injured, and some are killed. The first litters are born in late spring or early summer after a *gestation period* of 22 to 30 days. There are between 1 and 11 young in a litter, and the more northern-dwelling muskrats have about two litters a year. Muskrats are born helpless and blind but grow rapidly, and are on their own by the time they are one month old.

STATUS, SURVIVAL, AND MANAGEMENT

According to the Nunavut Wild Species 2000 report, the status of muskrats is *not assessed*. They are an important part of the Canadian fur industry. Predators in Nunavut include carnivores and birds. In the wild, they live 3 to 4 years, compared to 10 years in captivity.

DID YOU KNOW ?

When swimming under ice, the muskrat is reportedly able to refresh the air in its lungs by breathing in large bubbles of air trapped under the ice.

Brown Lemming
Lemmus trimucronatus

APPEARANCE

The brown lemming is a small, soft rodent. It has a reddish-brown back and rump with a grey head and shoulders. During the winter its coat is longer and greyer. It has a plump little body, a small head, and appears to have no neck. It has beady little eyes, and its small ears are almost hidden by its fur. It also has a small tail. The claws on its furry feet are adapted for digging. The soles of its feet and its toes are covered with long, stiff bristles. Considering the size of the brown lemming, it has a very large skull. The average length of a female is 14.5 cm and average weight is 68 g. The average length for the adult male is 15 cm and average weight is 78 g.

Paul Nicklen

FOOD AND FEEDING

Brown lemmings feed mostly on tender grass shoots. In addition, they eat tundra grass and sedge, as well as moss, bark, and twigs from dwarf willows and dwarf birch, berries, lichens, and roots.

BEHAVIOUR

Although lemmings live close together in colonies, they are not always very nice to each other. During mating season and when populations are very high, they fight amongst themselves. They squeal, box, and may even flip themselves onto their backs and try to bite their opponent. They swim easily, floating high in the water due to their soft, thick fur. They remain active during the 24-hour daylight periods, digging tunnels through the moss and tundra. During the winter, they are active beneath the snow. Spring and autumn are dangerous times for them, as they are more exposed to their many predators.

HABITAT

The ideal dwelling places for brown lemmings are wet tundra areas covered with grasses and sedges. They also live along stream-banks, lakeshores, grassy slopes, meadows, and rocky places.

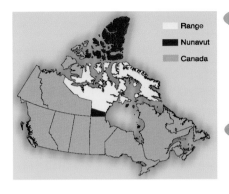

RANGE

The brown lemming can be found in southern Baffin Region, northern Kivalliq Region, and southwestern Kitikmeot Region.

REPRODUCTION

Females may have one to three litters a year. During high litter seasons, breeding may take place under the snow in the winter as well as during the summer, from mid-June to September. After a *gestation period* of 23 days, the female gives birth to between four and nine young.

STATUS, SURVIVAL, AND MANAGEMENT

According to the Nunavut Wild Species Report 2000, the status of brown lemmings is considered *secure*. The population's peaks and falls are directly related to a lack of food brought on by the large populations in the peak years. Brown lemmings generally live one or two years in the wild and up to three years in captivity. Predators in Nunavut include carnivores, birds, and even caribou.

DID YOU KNOW ?

Any opening that is big enough for a lemming's head is big enough for the whole body. Although they have fat little bodies, they can squeeze through amazingly small openings.

APPEARANCE

The Peary Land collared lemming is the only rodent that turns white in the winter, at which time it looks like a big cottonball. It has wide feet with heavily furred soles and long, stiff hairs sticking out around the toes. During the summer, its shoulders, chest, and legs are light to dark brown. It has a grey back with a black stripe down the middle and a light brown belly. Its fur is long and thick. The average length for males and females is between 13 and 16 cm, and the average weight is between 45 and 113 g.

R. Popko

FOOD AND FEEDING

The collared lemming feeds mainly on dwarf willow leaves and *forbs*, although it will also eat sedges, grasses, berries, buds, and twigs. Clumps of willows may be completely stripped after a year of high lemming populations.

BEHAVIOUR

R. Popko

This species has many of the same behaviours as brown lemmings. For example, they also hop around and shadowbox when cornered. Collared lemmings are active throughout the winter beneath the snow in their tunnels. During the summer they dig tunnels in the sod. These may be up to 2.5 m long, between 10 and 20 cm below ground, and between 5 and 7.5 cm in *diameter*. The family bonds are strong, and both parents care for the young. The whole family usually stays together until the young reach sexual maturity, at which time fathers may mate with their daughters.

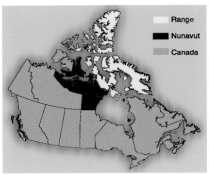

Range
Nunavut
Canada

HABITAT

The Peary Land collared lemming inhabits the Arctic tundra zone. In the summer, it lives in higher, rockier, drier areas than the brown lemming, but this really depends on the moisture conditions.

RANGE

The Peary Land collared lemming is found throughout Baffin Region and in the northeast portion of Kitikmeot Region.

REPRODUCTION

The breeding season usually begins in early March and lasts until early September. However, during a short time when their snow tunnels melt and they are busy digging their summer tunnels, they may not breed. Under the right winter conditions, breeding may start as early as January. Females are very aggressive during the breeding period. *Gestation* is between 19 and 21 days, but can be as long as 26 days due to *delayed implantation*. There are between one and seven offspring, with an average of five per litter. They are born blind and deaf and weigh about 3.8 g. By the end of the second week their eyes and ears are functional and they appear above ground shortly after. Males are mature at 46 days, and females at 27 to 30 days.

STATUS, SURVIVAL AND MANAGEMENT

According to the Nunavut Wild Species 2000 report, the status of the collared lemming is considered *undetermined*. Few collared lemmings live more than a year in the wild and just over three years in captivity. Predators in Nunavut include carnivores and birds.

OTHER SPECIES FOUND IN NUNAVUT

Other species of lemmings found in different parts of Nunavut that differ in appearance and range but have many similarities to the Peary Land collared lemming include the Victoria collared lemming and Richardson's collared lemming.

Lemming tunnels include different chambers. The ones used for nesting are lined with dry grasses and sometimes feathers and muskox wool. Some chambers are used as toilets.

When asked if she had ever heard about stars falling to the ground and going around in circles until they turned to lemmings or albino caribou, Rachel Ujarasuk shared the following:

I have never heard that they were the product of the stars that had fallen to the ground. What I have heard is that lemmings with claws that appear to be built up in layers are ones that have fallen from the heavens.

Also, after a recent snowfall you can see animal tracks easily but there are times when you come across these tracks and you cannot determine where they originated. You see that the tracks are spiral shaped and began from nowhere. Where the tracks began from the centre and worked their way out forming a spiral, it is believed they were caused by an animal that had just recently fallen from the heavens. The explanation or proof that was given was the fact that the tracks did not have a starting point. It was said that the animal would begin walking in a circle, forming a spiral and that the tracks eventually led away from this form.

When an animal fell down to earth from the heavens and the tracks worked themselves to the centre of the spiral by going around in circles, the animal would be found dead in the centre. I have heard that these animals had fallen down from the heavens but I have not heard that these were stars that had fallen to earth. I have seen these kinds of tracks on more than one occasion, the ones I have seen were those of a lemming. The claws of white lemmings (amirllak) are usually formed in layers and they used to say that these were the lemmings that had fallen from the heavens.

As youngsters we used to take the skins of small animals for us to play house with, so we used to look after them very well so that we could have them longer.

Rachel Ujarasuk, 1990

Meadow Vole
Microtus pennsylvanicus

APPEARANCE

Meadow voles have long, thick fur coats that range in colour from speckled rust-brown to dark brown on top and dusky grey below. The winter coat is longer and thicker than the summer coat. There is not a huge difference in size between the sexes. Males and females are generally between 15 and 20 cm in length and 30 to 50 g in weight.

A. Veitch

FOOD AND FEEDING

The meadow vole eats mostly tubers and green vegetation, including grasses and sedges. It will also eat seeds, grains, bark, fruits, insects, snails, and other invertebrates and vertebrates. It can eat more than its weight in food in one day.

BEHAVIOUR

The meadow vole is active all year, usually early in the morning and just before sunset. It creates a maze of tunnels through the grass that lead to shallow burrows. The nests inside the burrows are made of grass. During the winter, the nests are below the snow. Small piles of *feces* can be found some distance from the nest. The meadow vole appears to be clean mammal and does not *defecate* where it sleeps. The meadow vole makes noises to warn others of danger, and if alarmed, it will stamp its hind feet.

RANGE

In Nunavut, the meadow vole can be found in southern Kivalliq and Kitikmeot Regions.

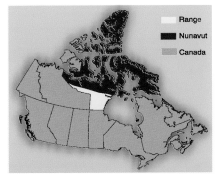

Range
Nunavut
Canada

HABITAT

The meadow vole inhabits wet meadow areas and open grassland near water. Good overhead grass cover is needed for both food and shelter.

A. Veitch

REPRODUCTION

Meadow voles have a very productive breeding life, producing litter after litter throughout April to October. If conditions are ideal, they may even breed all winter long. Between 1 and 11 young are born after a *gestation period* of about 21 days. Depending on the time of year, males generally reach maturity at 45 days, and females at 25 days.

STATUS, SURVIVAL, AND MANAGEMENT

According to the Nunavut Wild Species 2000 report, the status of the meadow vole is *not assessed*. Predators in Nunavut include carnivores and birds. The meadow vole usually lives for less than one year in the wild and up to a few years in captivity.

OTHER SPECIES FOUND IN NUNAVUT

Other species of voles found in different parts of Nunavut that differ in appearance and range but have many similarities to the meadow vole include the tundra vole, the yellow-cheeked vole, and the heather vole.

DID YOU KNOW ?

Like some other small mammals, the meadow vole will sometimes eat its own *fec* in order to absorb all possible nutrients and vitamins.

Northern Red-Backed Vole
Clethrionomys rutilus

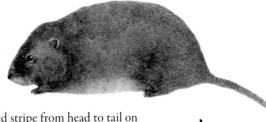

APPEARANCE

The northern red-backed vole is a small, some-what slender, brightly coloured vole. It has round, furry ears, and a short tail. In the win-ter, the fur is long and dense. The summer coat is shorter and coarser. It has an obvious wide red stripe from head to tail on its back. The face and sides are generally a yellowish-brown, and the belly varies between shades of grey to almost white. Males and females are generally the same size, with an average length of 15 cm and average weight of 22 g.

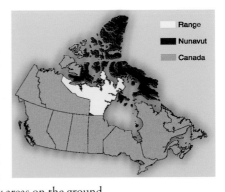

First Light

FOOD AND FEEDING

The red-backed vole feeds mainly on leaves, buds, twigs, and fruit from a wide range of shrubs. It also eats *forbs*, fungi, and insects, but does not eat mosses or lichens.

BEHAVIOUR

This species is *nocturnal*, but can be seen during twilight and dawn. In addition, it may need to remain active into daylight hours as the summer approaches and night becomes shorter or disappears completely. It stays active all winter, building tunnels under the snow and continuing to feed on roots and other vegetation.

RANGE

The red-backed vole can be found throughout Kivalliq Region and into parts of Kitikmeot and Baffin Regions.

HABITAT

In Nunavut, the red-backed vole inhabits rocky tundra as well as forested areas in the southern Kivalliq Region. It lives among shrubs and builds its nest in grassy areas on the ground.

	Range
	Nunavut
	Canada

REPRODUCTION

The breeding season is from May to August, and females can have up to three litters during the short season. Between four and nine young are born after a *gestation period* of 17 to 19 days. As with most rodents, the young are born blind, furless, greyish-pink, and deaf. Their growth is rapid, and by about the 18th day they leave the nest. Red-backed voles have an average lifespan of 10 to 12 months, with a maximum of 20 months.

STATUS, SURVIVAL AND MANAGEMENT

According to the Nunavut Wild Species 2000 Report, the status of northern red-backed voles is *undetermined*. They live about one year in the wild. Predators in Nunavut include carnivores, other rodents, and birds.

OTHER SPECIES FOUND IN NUNAVUT

Other voles that are found in parts of Nunavut include the tundra vole, the heather vole, and the yellow-cheeked vole.

DID YOU KNOW ?

Voles are a source of food for a variety of animals. They eat harmful insect larvae.

Arctic Ground Squirrel

Spermophilus parryii

APPEARANCE

The Arctic ground squirrel, or siksik, is the largest of all the ground squirrels, and also the most northern-dwelling squirrel. It has a cinnamon-coloured head, cheeks, shoulders, legs, and underparts. Its back is a speckled grey, black, and white. Its tail is a mix of brown- and black-tipped hairs. It has two annual *molts*, one in June and one in the autumn. The summer coat tends to be more reddish, and the winter coat, more greyish. The average length of a female is 38.5 cm and the average weight is generally 700 g. The average length of a male is 40 cm and the average weight is generally 800 g.

Paul Nicklen

FOOD AND FEEDING

The Arctic ground squirrel is *omnivorous*. It eats a variety of tundra vegetation such as leaves, seeds, stems, flowers, grass roots and fruit. In addition, it may eat *carrion*, eggs, other ground squirrels, and even some nesting birds.

BEHAVIOUR

Arctic ground squirrels are social animals that live in colonies. Adult squirrels may enter many different burrows; however, males will try to control an area that contains more than one female. They kill and eat young ground squirrels from other colonies. Not only does this provide the colony with food, it also increases the territory available to future generations. These squirrels wander the tundra and develop a little system of trails. They travel low to the ground, and if alarmed, will make a dash for their burrow. They are not afraid of water and will swim across small creek beds that get in their way. The permafrost of the Arctic limits ground squirrels to digging shallow tunnels and burrows. Their systems are extensive, sometimes having as many as 56 entrances in an area covering 46 m². The *diameters* of the burrows vary with the size of the squirrels, but are usually between 5 and 20 cm. Arctic ground squirrels hibernate for roughly seven months of the year. Their hibernation dens are specially constructed tunnels separate from the main burrow. They are usually between 60 and 76 cm below ground and are lined with a combination of grasses, lichens, leaves, and even some caribou or ground-squirrel hair. They roll themselves into a ball, tuck their heads in, wrap their tails over their heads and shoulders,

Paul Nicklen

and fall into a deep slumber. During hibernation, their body temperature drops by more than half, from 36.4°C to 17°C. They must have enough fat on them to last until April or May, when they first start emerging from their dens. When they emerge depends largely on geographic location and weather. Generally, the further north the squirrels live, the later they will emerge from their den. After they emerge, the squirrels feed on a *cache* of food they stored the summer before as they wait for fresh vegetation to begin growing.

RANGE

The Arctic ground squirrel can be found in Kivalliq Region, in the southern portion of Kitikmeot Region, and on Melville Peninsula in Baffin Region.

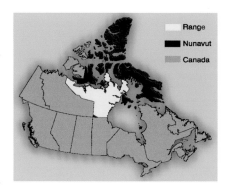

HABITAT

The habitat of the Arctic ground squirrel is limited by permafrost. In Nunavut, it is generally restricted to gravel or sandy hills, where the soil drains and prevents permafrost from developing near the surface. Some typical habitats also include *eskers*, *moraines*, riverbanks, lakeshores, and sand banks. In the more southern portions of its range, habitats include meadows.

REPRODUCTION

Arctic ground squirrels breed during a few weeks in the month of May. After a *gestation period* of about 25 days, they give birth to an average of six young. The young are completely helpless but develop quickly. Their eyes open after 20 days and they emerge from the den soon after to explore the environment immediately outside their dens. After a week, they slowly begin venturing further out. By late summer, they leave the family den and go out on their own, either finding and occupying an empty den or digging a new one. Many young ground squirrels die during their first winter, as their new dens either flood or are penetrated by permafrost. In an effort to gain enough fat to last them through the winter, the young have to stay active longer than the adults. They reach maturity during the following spring.

STATUS, SURVIVAL, AND MANAGEMENT

According to the Nunavut Wild Species 2000 report, the status of the Arctic ground squirrel is *secure*. The Arctic ground squirrel lives for a maximum of 8 to 10 years in the wild. Predators in Nunavut include humans, carnivores, and birds. Traditionally, the Arctic ground squirrel was used for food and a warm fur lining for the inside of parkas.

DID YOU KNOW ?

The Arctic ground squirrel, as you read above, eats a variety of food, including *carrion*. There is a record of one having carried away about 900 g of caribou meat during a single day!

Red Squirrel
Tamiasciurus hudsonicus

APPEARANCE

Red squirrels have small, round ears, a white ring around their eyes, thick, light brown coats, and long, reddish tails. They have a cream-coloured underbelly. Red squirrels have long claws on all four paws that allow them to climb and handle food easily. There is not a huge difference in size between the sexes. The average length and weight for an adult red squirrel is generally between 28 and 34 cm from nose to tip of tail and 130 and 250 g in weight.

Paul Nicklen

FOOD AND FEEDING

The red squirrel eats mainly seeds, nuts, and cones from conifer trees. It also eat buds, flowers, fruits, bark, mushrooms, sap, some insects, bird eggs, and mice.

BEHAVIOUR

The red squirrel is a high-energy animal that is constantly active during daylight hours. It is bold and courageous, defending its territory from intruders by stamping its feet, flicking its tail, and chattering noisily. It builds its nests out of leaves and twigs. The red squirrel is active all year long.

RANGE

In Nunavut, the red squirrel can be found in southern Kivalliq Region, following the tree line.

HABITAT

The red squirrel can be found in wooded environments, and may occasionally be found in swamps.

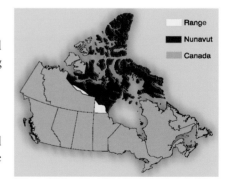

Range
Nunavut
Canada

REPRODUCTION

Breeding habits differ with latitude, but generally, between two and seven young are born after a *gestation period* of one to one and a half months. They are born helpless and hairless, but with well-developed claws. They appear out of the nest at about 10 weeks of age. Maturity is reached at one year.

STATUS, SURVIVAL, AND MANAGEMENT

According to the Nunavut Wild Species 2000 Report, the status of the red squirrel is *not assessed*. They have an approximate life span of 3 years in the wild and between 9 and 12 years in captivity. Predators in Nunavut include humans, carnivores, and birds. Several million red squirrels are trapped every year and used to line the inside of other fur garments.

OTHER SPECIES FOUND IN NUNAVUT

The porcupine is part of the family Erethizontidae. It can be found in a small portion of southern Kivalliq Region, following the tree line. It is popularly known for its unique quills, which serve as an effective defence against many potential predators.

DID YOU KNOW ?

Red squirrels do not hibernate. They build an extensive system of runways through the snow and stay busy all winter long.

Insectivora

Soricidae

Sorex cinereus

Wayne Van Devender

APPEARANCE

The masked shrew is among one of the smallest mammals in Nunavut. It has a long, pointed nose that never stops moving, tiny eyes and ears, delicate feet, and a fairly long tail. Brown on the back and silvery-white underneath, the masked shrew measures between 7 and 12.5 cm in length. Its weight is about four grams.

FOOD AND FEEDING

Masked shrews eat a variety of insects, some small mammals, seeds, larvae, mollusks, and vegetable matter. Shrews have a very high *metabolism* that means that they must eat often in order to survive. Masked shrews generally eat their weight in food every day. When females are pregnant, they will eat up to three times their weight in food.

BEHAVIOUR

Masked shrews have huge appetites and are almost constantly active. Other than a few one-hour rest periods, these shrews are busy 24 hours a day, all year long. They mostly hunt in burrows beneath the snow; however, their tracks can occasionally be seen on the snow. Shrews are not very friendly with one another. Siblings sometimes show *cannibalistic behaviour*, and the only time females tolerate males being around is during the breeding season. They make little twittering noises as they look for food, and when they are angry they make a quick series of high-pitched sounds.

HABITAT

The masked shrew prefers living in the margins of moist fields, moist or dry woods, willow and alder thickets, and brushlands.

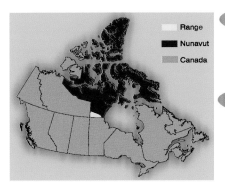

Range
Nunavut
Canada

RANGE

Masked shrews are found in southern Kivalliq Region.

REPRODUCTION

Not a lot is known about the reproduction of shrews. The breeding period is thought to last from late April to late September or October. Females have one or two litters a season. The *gestation period* for masked shrews is between 17 and 28 days, after which 2 to 10 young are born into a nest of grass. They are helpless at birth and develop slowly.

STATUS, SURVIVAL, AND MANAGEMENT

According to the Nunavut Wild Species 2000 report, the current status of masked shrews is *not assessed*. They live between 14 and 16 months and are preyed upon by larger shrews, weasels, hawks, and owls.

OTHER SPECIES IN NUNAVUT

Other species of shrews occasionally found in the southern portion of Kivalliq Region which have many similarities to the masked shrew include; the dusky shrew, arctic shrew and the pygmy shrew. Most closely related to the masked shrew and occurring in portions of southern Kivalliq Region is the barrenground shrew. It is found in wet sedge-grass meadows and dwarf willow and birch clumps.

DID YOU KNOW ?

No one is sure how many species of shrews exist because new species continue to be recognized.

Chiroptera

Vespertilionidae

Little Brown Bat
Myotis lucifugus

APPEARANCE

The little brown bat is one of the most common bats in Canada. This small species has a brown coat with long, coppery hairs on its back and a greyish stomach. All species have the ability to walk and have long legs. The wingspan is broad, and as with other bats in this family, the fingers have *evolved* to become very long in order to support the wing *membrane*. The size of the little brown bat is usually between 8 and 9.5 cm long, and it weighs between 5 and 12 g.

FOOD AND FEEDING

Little brown bats feed primarily on soft-bodied insects, especially flies and moths. They also feed on some hard beetles where available. They feed at a rate of seven to eight insects per minute.

Merlin D. Tuttle

BEHAVIOUR

As with other bats, little brown bats have the amazing ability to use *echolocation*. This allows them to fly through heavily forested terrain in the dark and to locate moths and insects from a distance. They have winter and summer roosts and may travel many miles to arrive at a suitable winter roost. Wintering takes place in caves and mines, as well as attics, old sheds, and other human-made spots. There may be a few bats or up to 300,000 bats in one cave.

HABITAT

The little brown bat lives in caves, mine tunnels, and hollow trees. It has adapted to urban life and uses a variety of buildings as roosting sites.

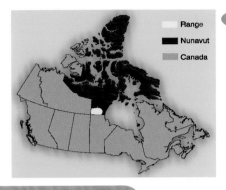

Range
Nunavut
Canada

RANGE

The little brown bat, and bats in general, are not commonly seen in Nunavut, as they are mostly forest dwellers. They follow the tree line into the southern portion of Kivalliq Region, and at times have been seen roosting a little farther north in man-made structures.

REPRODUCTION

Mating takes place in late summer and early autumn, when both sexes mate with several partners. Shortly thereafter, *torpor* sets in, and the bats are still for the winter. Following this period of *delayed implantation*, females ovulate in the spring and move to daytime roosts or maternity dens. They give birth to one or (rarely) two young after a *gestation period* of up to two months. The young can fly after three weeks. Females reach maturity at 12 months, and males at 14 months. Adult males are generally solitary during the spring and summer.

STATUS, SURVIVAL, AND MANAGEMENT

According to the Nunavut Wild Species 2000 report, the current status of the little brown bat is *sensitive*. It can live for 24 to 30 years in the wild. Its main predators in Nunavut include some carnivores and birds.

OTHER SPECIES FOUND IN NUNAVUT

The Canadian Museum of Nature collected a specimen of the eastern red bat in Coral Harbour in 1954. This is quite extraordinary as its range is generally limited to the southern portion of Canada.

DID YOU KNOW ?

Bats help stop insect populations from getting too big.

Hoary Bat
Lasiurus cinereus

APPEARANCE

The hoary bat's coat is dark brown with silver frosting on the back. The fur grows as far as the base of the wings and completely covers the *membrane* between the *femurs*. There is no fur on the underside of the wings. The belly area is covered with light brown, woolly fur, and there is also a patch at the base of the thumb and on the throat. The total length for a male and female is usually between 13 and 14.5 cm. The average wingspan is about 40 cm and average weight is usually 26 g. The hoary bat is the largest bat found in Canada.

FOOD AND FEEDING

The hoary bat feeds mostly on moths, although it will also eat dragonflies occasionally.

Merlin D. Tuttle

BEHAVIOUR

The hoary bat is *nocturnal*, and usually lives a solitary life. On occasion, it has been seen hunting in groups or roosting in a cave with other bats; however, these are generally considered exceptions. The hoary bat lives mainly in trees, sleeping among the leaves during the day and emerging only late into the night. It wraps its wings around its body to conserve heat.

HABITAT

The hoary bat lives in wooded areas, particularly coniferous forests. It is most often seen hunting over lakes or open areas.

Hoary Bat

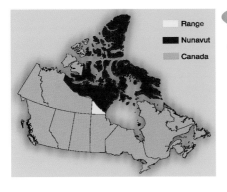

RANGE

The hoary bat can be found throughout the US and southern Canada. It roughly follows the tree line at its northern limit. Rare sightings have occurred above the tree line. These may be due to the bat's habit of roosting in shipping crates and being transported to places where it would not usually be found. Sightings in Arviat and Coral Harbour could be a result of this habit. Hoary bats are a migratory species and travel as far as the southern US and Bermuda.

REPRODUCTION

Very little is known about the reproductive cycle of hoary bats. It is thought that mating takes place in August and birth sometime in mid-June of the following year. The *gestation period* is believed to be 40 days, which means these bats have a long period of *delayed implantation*. Between one and four young are born per litter. Young hoary bats weigh approximately 4.5 g at birth. When they are older, they roost alongside their mother in a favourite spot. By the time they are one month old, they learn to fly and fend for themselves.

STATUS, SURVIVAL, AND MANAGEMENT

According to the Nunavut Wild Species 2000 report, the current status of the hoary bat is *undetermined*. Its main predators in Nunavut include some carnivores and birds.

DID YOU KNOW ?

Scientists believe that bats *evolved* from shrews.

Glossary

Alpha:	The most dominant individual in a same-sex group.
Bio-accumulation:	The accumulation of substances in the tissues of an organism.
Biomass:	The total mass of living matter within a given unit of environmental area.
Boss:	A circular bump or knob-like swelling, as on the horns of certain animals.
Browse:	To feed on leaves, young shoots, and other vegetation; graze.
Cache:	A hidden storage place.
Canine:	One of the pointed teeth on each side of the upper and lower jaws of an organism.
Cannibalistic behaviour:	An organism that feeds on others of its kind.
Canopy:	The uppermost portion of a forest, made up of the tops of trees.
Carrion:	The dead and rotting body of an animal.
Colour phases:	The different colours of an animal's fur over a period of time.
Defecate:	To empty the bowels.
Delayed implantation:	When the egg is fertilized but is not implanted in the uterus until later.
Dewlap:	A fold of loose skin hanging from the neck of some animals.
Diameter:	The length of a straight line passing through the center of a circle.
Disperse:	To separate and move in different directions.
DNA (deoxyribonucleic acid):	A nucleic acid that carries genetic information in a cell.
Echolocation:	Bats find out the location of something by measuring the time it takes for an echo to return from it.
Esker:	A long, narrow bridge of coarse gravel left by a stream flowing in or under a decaying glacial ice sheet.
Evolutionary process:	How living things change over a period of time.
Evolve:	To develop or arise through an evolutionary process. To develop and change through time.
Feces:	Waste matter eliminated through the bowels; excrement.
Femur:	The thigh bone.
Forb:	A broad-leafed herb other than grass, especially one found in an open area.
Gestation period:	The period during which an embryo develops.
Guard hairs:	The long, coarse hairs that form a layer that cover and protect the soft under-fur of certain animals.
Herbivore:	An animal that feeds mainly on plant matter.
Hierarchy:	A ranking or classification from lower to higher.
Incisors:	Teeth for cutting or gnawing located in the front of the mouth in both jaws.
Juvenile:	Not fully grown or developed; young.

Membrane:	A pliable sheet of tissue that covers or lines or connects organs or cells of animals.
Metabolism:	The series of chemical changes that take place in an organism, by means of which food is manufactured and utilized and waste materials are eliminated.
Molt:	To shed or cast off a bodily covering.
Moraines:	An accumulation of boulders, stones, or other debris carried and deposited by a glacier.
Muzzle:	The long front part of an animals head that includes the mouth, nose and jaws; also called the snout.
Nocturnal:	Active during the night.
Not assessed:	The definition provided by the Nunavut Wild Species Report 2000 for not assessed is: species which have not been examined for this report.
Omnivorous:	An animal that feeds on both animal and vegetable matter.
PCBs	Polychlorinated biphenyl. PCBs are any family of industrial compounds produced by chlorination of biphenyl, which is noted mainly as an environmental pollutant that accumulates in animal tissue and results in various defects.
Qiviut:	The soft fur found on a muskox.
Radioactive fallout:	The harmful radiation given off when the nucleus of an atom breaks down; generally caused by atomic weapons testing.
Rendez-vous:	A meeting place.
Retract:	To draw or take back in.
Rut:	Mating season for caribou.
Scavenge:	To search through garbage or leftovers for food or something useful.
Scavenger:	An individual that searches through garbage or leftovers for food or something useful.
Secure:	The definition provided by the Nunavut Wild Species Report 2000 for secure is: species which are not at risk or sensitive.
Semi-retractable:	To be able to pull back in, part of the way.
Sensitive:	The definition provided by the Nunavut Wild Species Report 2000 for sensitive is: species which are not at risk of extinction or extirpation but may require special attention or protection to prevent them from becoming at risk.
Snout:	The long front part of an animal's head that includes the nose, mouth and jaws; also called the muzzle.
Sustainable harvest:	The collection of species without depleting their populations.
Torpor:	A state of mental and motor inactivity generally found in hibernating animals.
Under-fur:	The soft coat of fur that grows next to the skin that is usually covered with guard hairs in animals.
Undetermined:	The definition provided by the Nunavut Wild Species Report 2000 for undetermined is; species for which insufficient information, knowledge, or data is available to reliably evaluate their general status.
Weaned:	When an organism stops drinking its mother's milk and finds its nutrition from other sources.

Bibliography

Banfield, A.W.F. (1974). The Mammals of Canada. Toronto: University of Toronto Press.

Banfield, A.W.F. (1961). A Revision of the Reindeer and Caribou, Genus Rangifer. Ottawa: Queen's Printer and Controller of Stationary.

Forsyth, A. (1999). Mammals of North America: Temperate and Arctic Regions. Buffalo, New York: Firefly Books (US) Inc.

Graves, J., & Hall, E. (1998). Arctic Animals. NWT: Department Of Culture and Communications, Publications and Production Division.

Halfpenny, J. (1986). A Field Guide to Mammal Tracking in North America. Boulder, Colorado, USA: Johnson Printing Company.

Ijjiraq, A. (1990, March 11). Igloolik Oral History Project Interview. IE 121.

Innuksuk, A. (1986, October 28). Igloolik Oral History Project Interview. IE 004.

Kappianaq, G. (1997, August 21). Igloolik Oral History Project Interview. IE 408.

Kunnuk, P. (1990, November 22). Igloolik Oral History Project Interview. IE 162.

Piugaattuk, M. K. (1991, February 7). Igloolik Oral History Project Interview. IE 182.

Piugaattuk, N. (1991, January 30). Igloolik Oral History Project Interview. IE 177.

---. (1989, March 6). Igloolik Oral History Project Interview. IE 050.

Richard, P. (2001) Marine Mammals of Nunavut. Nunavut: Department of Education, Q.S.O.

Baffin Divisional Board of Education. (1997). Birds of Nunavut. Nunavut: Baffin Divisional Board of Education.

Government of Nunavut. (2000) Nunavut Wild Species 2000, General Status on Wild Species in Nunavut. Nunavut: Government of Nunavut, Department of Sustainable Development.

RWED. (1999). NWT Wildlife Sketches, 4rth edition. Yellowknife.

Qulaut, E. (1990, March 8). Igloolik Oral History Project Interview. IE 133.

Interviews cited from the Igloolik Oral History Project are held by the Nunavut Research Institute, Igloolik, NU, and at the Prince of Wales Heritage Centre, Yellowknife, NWT.

WEBSITES

Environment Canada has various websites that provide information on various species of wildlife found in Canada:
> (http://www.speciesatrisk.gc.ca/species/English/SearchRequest.cfm)
> (http://www.cws-scf.ec.gc.ca/hww-fap/index_e.cfm)

University of Michigan Museum of Zoology, Animal Diversity Web is a website that provides information on various species of wildlife:
> (http://animaldiversity.ummz.umich.edu/index.html)

Government of the Northwest Territories, Resources, Wildlife and Economic Development is a website that provides information on various species of wildlife:
> (http://www.nwtwildlife.rwed.gov.nt.ca/NWTwildlife/nwtwildlife.htm)

Science Made Simple Inc. is a website that provides information on metric conversions:
> (http://www.sciencemadesimple.com/conversions.html)

Dictionary.com is a website that provides information on various aspects of language use:
> (http://www.dictionary.com/)

Citation Styles Online! Is a website that provides information on various citation styles:
> (http://www.bedfordstmartins.com/online/citex.html)

WENGER DATABASE - Igloolik Research Institute

Anderson, Rudolf Martin. (1924). Report on the Natural History Collections of the Expedition. In Vilhjalmur Stefansson, My Life with the Eskimo. New York: Macmillan, pp. 501-502, 507.

PHOTOGRAPHS

Paul Nicklen Photography, Whitehorse, YT
Eyewire
Department of Sustainable Development, Government of Nunavut
Alastair Veitch, RWED
Richard Popko, RWED
Merlin D. Tuttle, Bat Conservation International
Nick Newberry
First Light Associated Photographers Inc.
Hans L.- Blohm
Wayne Van Devender
Noah Oqaituq
Patrick J. Endres/AlaskaPhotoGraphics